SOLOMON'S
WISDOM FOR
WOMEN

SOLOMON'S WISDOM FOR WOMEN

Grady M Sanders Jr

Library of Congress Control Number:		2021904502
ISBN:	Hardcover	978-1-6641-6175-7
	Softcover	978-1-6641-6174-0
	eBook	978-1-6641-6173-3

Print information available on the last page.

Rev. date: 03/08/2021

To order additional copies of this book, contact:
Xlibris
844-714-8691
www.Xlibris.com
Orders@Xlibris.com
819252

This book is dedicated to the one true God.

In honor of my mother, Lillie M. Sanders, who gave me life; my wife, Cherette J. Sanders, who gives me joy; my daughter, Renee E. Perry; and my sisters, aunts, nieces, female cousins, and all other women, for they are all recipients of God's love. To all these people, I say thank you.

Sorrow's Smile

There is no wisdom in sorrow,
There is neither understanding,
But there is remembrance of a smile a laugh a look a word or a voice,
And then there is your smile and yes there is joy in sorrow,
In remembering your loved one or friend.

CONTENTS

Preface

Purpose and Theme

One day as I thought about the book of Proverbs, I wondered if women read Proverbs and could they relate the teachings therein to their lives seeing that it was addressed to men. Did they perceive or attempt to understand this book of the Bible as they did the other books of the Bible and thought to give some consideration to it and derive meaning from Solomon's words and attempt to apply them to their everyday lives as well? I then thought to write this paraphrased edited version of the proverbs of Solomon. Since the Word of God, in my opinion, whether written or spoken in any version, is good for understanding, I chose to use the King James Version of the Bible as my version of choice and use it as the framework from which to create and share this work and direct it mainly toward women in an attempt to provide them a similar understanding of the shared knowledge of Solomon's proverbs for them. By undertaking this effort, I am hoping to provide to women a different form of source material for them to relate to God from their own individual perspectives so that they may have a feeling of inclusiveness and closeness to God. I am not making any attempt to insinuate that I know how a woman thinks, not being of the same mind, nor am I insinuating that I know how a woman should or should not act, but I am attempting to give women an opportunity to relate the writings of Proverbs to their physical and spiritual lives.

As my daughter grew into a young adult, I attempted to speak with her about some of life's experiences and wanted to give her some guidance by pointing out to her visually as we went on errands and to events or just traveled around as a family, that the people she could meet in different situations in which she could get involved in be it knowingly or unknowingly along with some of them trouble could follow which may come with those encounters. I also asked her to look at the people that lived on the street where they were and what they were doing and how they may have gotten there, be they homeless or not. I told her that people may ask her to do things be they interesting or not and as I tried to explain how some got to where are by making the wrong decisions. So I put a question to her. Like what are you going to do to make yourself a success or would you like to be a failure, and your joy depends on the type of life decisions you make, and by letting her know, simply put that she could choose to be a failure or a success. Therefore, I did the best I could in sharing with her my own limited wisdom since there was not much material out there of this sort that I could share with her in the beginning. I knew that I could not be with her every moment, so I'd hoped to give her something else besides self-help materials to remind her of the things that she would encounter in life. And I know that any parent may feel the same way not only for their daughter but also for their son. As I considered some of the things I shared with my daughter, I then revisited the idea and set out to make a relevant version of the proverbs of Solomon and relate it to women by changing the male reference pronouns to the female form of pronouns, and with that came more changes to provide an easier-to-read book.

However, my aim is not to change any of the true meaning of Proverbs but to have for women a bit of source material that they can use as a reference with other materials. All women need to feel that the writing of Proverbs does include them even in its original form (so do read this version side by side with your version of choice) and to simply understand that wisdom is more than just something for men, that they can also have it as well. Therefore, I wanted this book to reflect that and envisioned for its title to be *Solomon's Wisdom for Women*. I thereby wrote this manuscript and intended to provide a self-help version to women. My thinking is that if Solomon had a daughter, whether he would have written to her in a similar fashion, would he advise her on the diversity of life and its many nuances that are so interchangeable and at times hard to distinguish a good and peaceable way of life, which can be both moral and just, as he did in instructing his son. And if he had a daughter, would he advise her to also be a success with and in her life and her family.

Women should also feel that their success brings the same values to their families, including their sons and husbands, as well as their daughters. Men should also read the book of Proverbs for similar reasons. God's expectation is for men and women to obtain wisdom on how to grow and live together. And by obtaining understanding, women can come to know their self-worth and abilities and qualities, which lie within them, to aid them in being a more spiritual and successful person and for them to be of help to other women so that we all may continually seek grace through knowledge and wisdom daily.

As with any new generation, there are changes in society that cause attitudes to differ from one generation to another, so I wanted to keep *Solomon's Wisdom for Women* as relevant as possible and to keep the overall intent of its meaning closely related to the original meaning as a base and relate it to our current society just as Solomon did. As with each new generation, the precepts and ideas may change, but the foundational structures remain the same. So I thought to make Solomon's Wisdom *for Women* a source of inspiration similar to what men have when they look to read the proverbs of Solomon for the purpose of knowing wisdom and obtaining guidance for life's challenges.

I like to believe that as a wise man, although I am no wiser than any man and surely not as wise as Solomon was, my hope is that this paraphrased version will make a difference in the lives of the people who read it. Therefore *Solomon's Wisdom for Women* is meant to be an unchanging guide in a similar manner as Solomon's proverbs. I am not asking that the words I am penning are not to be changed or paraphrased in some manner and should not be rewritten in another form, for I know that they can and should be. After all, I did the same with Proverbs from the KJV and other versions. People may rewrite it, just as I did with their version of choice, which is great for the advancement of people and their relationships. However, the intent of this manuscript is for it to be similar to what the original writer of the King James Version wrote regarding his words. And I hope it will be remembered in its current form today and thereafter, for that is how I intended for this work to be, just a simple version of the original writings as a guide.

1

The Usefulness of Wisdom

[1] The Wisdom of Solomon, the son of David, king of Israel:

[2] My daughter, obtaining knowledge will help you comprehend the nature of things. Along with wisdom comes instruction, perception, and understanding; therefore, a lot can be accomplished.

[3] Therefore, by receiving the instructions that wisdom provides, there are opportunities for justice, judgment, and fairness with equity. Additionally, disciplined learning can improve your quality of life.

[4] Receiving wisdom, whether subtly or openly, will enable prudent practices for a young woman so that she can gain knowledge and personal discretion.

[5] A wise woman can hear and increase knowledge through learning, and a woman's comprehension will endure over time. And by being attentive to wise counsel from wise women, a woman can avoid many pitfalls.

[6] My daughter, to know a proverb's secret meaning, you must meditate on it.

[7] My daughter, the fear of the Lord is the beginning of knowledge to keep you from danger, but the foolish woman will despise wisdom and instruction and go into unfamiliar woods, not having learned to avoid danger.

❧ Sinful Enticements ❧

[8] A daughter should listen to her father's words and not forsake the words of her mother, which are like laws.

[9] Their teachings shall be an ornament of grace upon your head, like a tiara, and a gold pendant worn about your neck.

[10] My daughter, if sinners entice you to go with them, do not give in and do not consent to unjust acts.

[11] They will say unto you, "Come with us. Let us lay waiting to commit crimes. Also, let us hide and lurk about for the innocent for no reason other than for pleasure,"

[12] They will also entice you by saying, "We will swallow them up alive. We shall devour them as grapes. It will be as if they fell into an open grave, or as rabbits trapped in a snare.

[13] We shall find the venerable out in the open, thereby taking all their precious substances, and we shall fill our houses with their spoils."

[14] My daughter, do not give in or promise to commit crimes just to be considered a part of their family and remain as an equal.

[15] My daughter, choose not to walk the same path as they do; choose rather to refrain from walking in any deviant way.

[16] Many girls go swiftly to run a crooked path in their search to shed innocent blood.

[17] Surely it is vain to spread a net in the sight of any bird, yet some will be tempted and will fall into an open snare, so beware.

[18] And they who lay waiting to commit evil will find others lurking privately for their lives because they do not consider that they will reap injustice to themselves.

[19] Therefore, she who is contemplating stealing has the same feelings as all others. Her desire to be deceitful and to steal in order to obtain riches seems just, but what she does not know is that tainted riches will take away the dignity of the people who owns stolen property.

❧ The Voice of Wisdom ❧

[20] Wisdom cries without; she utters her voice in the streets. Are you listening to her call?

[21] When wisdom shouts her words in the middle of the square, where there are many opportunities at the opening of different venues around the city,

[22] Wisdom says, "How long, ye simple ones? Will ye love ignorance and hate knowledge?" There will always be scorners who delight in their hatred of honest people and pure things, and some will have contempt for those who use wisdom.

[23] Wisdom says, "Behold, I will pour out my spirit unto you, and I will cause you to know and understand how wisdom affects your life. Therefore, turn not away from my words as I rebuff you for your actions and do not continue onward onto what may be considered a dark place."

[24] Wisdom speaks and asks, "Why refuse me? I have stretched out my hand, and you did not reach for it. Neither should you refuse my appeal.

[25] Why have you rejected all my counsel, and why would you not receive any of my instructions intended to aid you?"

[26] Therefore says wisdom, "I cannot but laugh at your calamity. And I will not be of any help to you. I will mock you when your fear comes because your personal wisdom may not be as strong.

[27] And when your fear regarding failure comes at a delicate time and destruction comes as a whirlwind, resulting in distress and anguish, do not ask why.

[28] When you attempt to recall your words of wisdom, but like a room filled with rags, you will find nothing useful. Because you looked for me too late, you were unable to find a way from under your dilemma."

[29] All because that you hated knowledge, denying its good counsel, and did not choose the fear of the Lord.

³⁰ And she would not travel in any of the paths that wisdom's counsel provided, she also despised the influence of wisdom and instead chose fun and folly.

³¹ Therefore, they shall look upon her who chose to eat of the fruit of her own judgment and go her own way by despising my counsel and using the schemes of others, which became the thread of her undoing.

³² My daughter, in order for the simple to turn away from the right path and bring havoc upon themselves, they have to be complacent, covetous, and give in to slothfulness. That is how they enslaved their soul.

³³ But whosoever listens to me shall dwell safely and shall be a recipient of a quiet spirit and be at peace from fear of evil.

³⁴ My daughter, there are some spirits that speak having wisdom and some that speak, out of turn, having none and some will speak lies rejecting the truth. What type of spirit are you willing to have?

2

The Value in Wisdom

¹ My daughter, if you will receive my words and hide my commandments in the treasure chest that is your heart

² And will be inclined to give me your attention in order to receive wisdom and apply your strength toward having a strong spirit, then will you come to know and have understanding?

³ Surely, if you ask for knowledge and wisdom like a thirst for water and raise up your voice to call for understanding,

⁴ If you seek for the knowledge of wisdom as silver and search for her as a treasure hidden in a field,

⁵ Then you will understand the fear of the Lord emanating from your spirit, then your spirit shall find that the knowledge of God has always been with you.

⁶ For Adonai gives wisdom, thereby out of His mouth comes knowledge and understanding straight into your heart.

⁷ He gives to the righteous woman as a reward sound wisdom because He is a buckler for her that walks upright and with integrity.

⁸ With judgment, He keeps the paths of righteousness from error and will also preserve the way of saintly women who walk within the defined paths of righteousness.

⁹ Then you shall understand the paths of righteousness, judgment, and equity. Yes, and you will recognize every good path and take it.

¹⁰ When wisdom enters your heart like food toward the satisfying of the belly, then know that knowledge is also sweet and pleasant to the mind and the soul.

¹¹ Discretion and purity shall preserve you, and understanding shall keep you in your travels.

¹² Good judgment will deliver you from the ways of evil, from the person who speaks negative and deceitful things into your ear, for there is no other way for wickedness to work its way toward your heart and to lead you astray.

¹³ Wisdom is a good guide and will not lead you from the paths of uprightness, nor will it enable you to walk in the ways of darkness.

¹⁴ Many foolish women rejoice to do evil and delight in the deceitfulness of those who practice living in the spur of the moment and find delight doing so.

¹⁵ Because their paths are all so crooked, therefore they will have a conflicting spirit and they will go willingly with the thing that will divert them from their path in order to rejoice in more wickedness.

❧ Wicked Men ❧

¹⁶ Wisdom is nearby and attempts to speak to you in order to deliver you from the craftiness of strange men, even from the stranger who flatters with his words.

¹⁷ Know that he has forsaken the guidance of his father's words and his mother's instructions, which were given in his youth; he also chooses not to remember the covenant between him and his God.

¹⁸ His house is inclined to be deceitful and hides a spider's snare; it also leads to sheol, for many have died from just considering to walk with him and partaking of his indulgences.

¹⁹ None who goes with him shall return again to fruitfulness; neither will they again be able to take hold of their original path of life.

❦ A Stable Woman ❦

20 My daughter, in order for you to continue to walk in the ways of godly women and to be kept in the paths of the righteous, be wise.

21 In order for a woman to maintain a secure connection with those things that are important, let her take heed to wisdom, for it will allow the perfect to remain, but wickedness does separate the righteous woman from her God.

22 Therefore, she who is wicked shall be cut off from the perfect place, and for her transgressions, she shall be uprooted out of the land and into seclusion away from the righteous.

23 My daughter, evil is deceitful and dwells nearby, and it is known to have a voice.

3

Using Wisdom

[1] My daughter, forget not my law and do not take it lightly, but let your heart and mind keep my commandments and let them be more than a thoughtful suggestion.

[2] The instructions of wisdom will enable you to have many great, pleasant, and fruitful days, along with a healthy and long life. Wisdom shall add peace to your soul.

[3] Let not the spirit of mercy and truth be foreign to you. It's OK for a leaf to lose its connection to a branch, but for your spirit to lose its connection to Adonai is death to the soul. Along with mercy and truth, allow love and forgiveness to rest upon the table of your heart.

[4] Then surely you shall find favor and good understanding with women and men in the sight of God.

[5] A woman who trusts in the Lord with all her heart and leans not totally on her own understanding will not utterly fail.

[6] She who acknowledges God in all her ways is sure of herself, because she knows that He always direct the paths of righteous women.

[7] Be not wise in your own eyes when you look in the mirror for admiration, but fear the Lord and depart from evil quickly.

[8] Because wisdom can be like a healing herb for your mind and like marrow in your bones, that, along with a stout and firm soul, can bring peace to your thoughts.

⁹ Honor the Lord with all your substance, which you have gained from labor, along with the first fruits of all your increase.

¹⁰ Then Adonai shall fill your barns with diverse fruits for you to prosper therewith, and as your winepresses fill, they shall burst to enrich others.

¹¹ My daughter, despise not the chastening of the Lord; neither be weary of His attempts to guide you in decision-making, to add light instead of bewilderment, correction instead of reproof.

¹² And she who is loved by the Lord will be chastised with His love, as a father corrects the inactions of the daughter in whom he delights.

❧ Seeking Wisdom and Its Benefits ❧

¹³ Happy is the woman who finds wisdom, and for the woman who understands, she is enthusiastic and joyful.

¹⁴ For the merchandise of wisdom is better than the merchandise of silver, and the gain thereof is better than fine gold because it cannot be bargained for.

¹⁵ Wisdom is more precious than rubies, and none of the things that you have or you can desire can be compared to her.

¹⁶ The length of days is in her right hand, and in her left hand, riches and honor.

¹⁷ Her ways are ways of pleasantness, and all her paths are peaceful.

¹⁸ She can be like a tree of life to a woman, because it is available for her to depend on. She who lays hold upon her shall obtain spiritual fruit and will be nourished as long as she retains her.

¹⁹ The Lord by His wisdom has founded the earth; by understanding, he has established the heavens, and He is capable of guiding you with His hand.

²⁰ By His knowledge, the depths are broken up and the clouds leave behind the dew.

²¹ My daughter, let not wisdom and understanding depart from before your eyes; keep sound wisdom and discretion forever within your reach.

²² Wisdom is graceful, and like pearls that adorn your neck, it adds beauty to your thoughts and is good for righteous purposes.

²³ Wisdom shall cause you to walk safely and securely daily, and your foot shall not stumble as often.

²⁴ When you rest, you shall not be afraid. Yea, you shall lie down, and your sleep shall be sweet.

²⁵ My daughter, be not afraid of sudden disaster and do not fear when destruction comes for the wicked, for when it comes, it is not for you.

²⁶ For the Lord shall be your confidence, and He shall keep your footing stable and keep you from being trapped.

²⁷ Withhold not that which is good from them to whom it is due, when it is within your power to do so.

²⁸ Say not unto your neighbor "Go and come back tomorrow" when you have it within your power to meet that need.

²⁹ Devise not evil against your neighbor; she trusts you because she believes that she dwells securely beside you.

³⁰ Strive not with a woman without a cause if she has done you no harm.

³¹ My daughter, envy not the oppressor nor desire her ways. By her actions, she invites trouble and much strife, so do not become too familiar with her spirit.

³² All the contrary souls are an abomination to the Lord, but He shares His secrets with the righteous as He is intimate with them and desires to be so with you.

³³ The curse of the Lord is in the house of the wicked, but He blesses the habitations of holy and just women.

³⁴ Surely He applies scorn to the scorners who defile His way, but to those who are saintly and kind and not overly vain are known to walk in His ways. He shall grant unto them grace.

³⁵ The wise woman shall inherit glory with grace, but for her who is a fool, she shall be promoted with shame and reclusiveness.

³⁶ She who has a heavy heart and whose soul is naked and open does not have the friendship that wisdom provides.

4

Love the Ways of Wisdom

¹ Hear, my daughter, the instruction of your father in order to gather some meaning and hope for life. Be attentive, and you shall have understanding.

² Therefore, I will provide to you good doctrine, so forsake not my principles for other teachings that do not profit.

³ I was cared for by my father because he knew I needed guidance. However, I was always sweet and beloved in the sight of my mother who is also wise and showed me the ways of a godly woman.

⁴ My father said unto me, "Let your heart retain my words and keep my commandments and live." My mother also spoke to me about kindness.

⁵ Get for yourself wisdom, O daughter, and obtain understanding and forget not their song. Neither decline from the written word, for it is a gift, and do not decline from my precepts or your mother's attempts to share with you how to be a saintly woman.

⁶ Therefore, forsake not wisdom's guidance because it shall provide a stable life for you. Love her, and she shall preserve and keep you.

⁷ Wisdom is the principal thing; therefore, obtain wisdom. It shall come with understanding, for they are like companions—lose one, lose both.

⁸ Exalt her, and she shall promote you. She shall bring you to honor; when you reach out to embrace her, it will be great for you.

⁹ Wisdom shall crown your head with an ornament of grace; a tiara of glory she shall deliver unto to you.

¹⁰ O my daughter, in order for the years of your life to be many, listen and receive my sayings.

¹¹ I have been teaching you in the ways of prudence, but in order for you to walk within the right paths, use wisdom.

¹² As you go about and walk upon the pathways of life, your steps shall not all be sure, for you will stumble but remain upright in your spirit.

¹³ Take fast hold of instruction and let her not go. Keep her close, for she is your life's companion and will help to direct you.

¹⁴ Enter not into the path of the wicked woman; neither should you go nor lean in the direction of wayward women.

¹⁵ In order for you to avoid wickedness and evil, one thing to do is to stop and ponder that which is before you and study it, pass by and turn from it, then go on your way.

¹⁶ Many women will not sleep, except they have done some wicked mischief; their spirit will not rest or sleep, unless they also cause someone to fail.

¹⁷ For they live to eat the bread of wickedness and will drink the wine of violence.

¹⁸ But the path of the just has a light that shines upon it, and that light shines brighter and brighter, leading you toward a perfect day.

¹⁹ The ways of the wicked are like different types of darkness. and for the purpose of carnal pleasure, they try new things springing from that darkness, Therefore they do not know which one causes them to stumble,.

²⁰ My daughter, attend to my words. Turn your attention toward my sayings and imitate them.

²¹ Let them not depart from before your eyes and stay focused; keep them in the midst of your heart.

²² For they are life unto all those who use them and can be health to all the flesh of women, keeping them away from many diseases.

❧ The Spiritual Heart ❧

[23] There is no heart that is more precious and dear than your own. Guard it because out of it comes the issues of life, and with all that is dear to your heart, keep with all diligence and be vigilant.

[24] Put away from you an angry spirit combined with perverse lips; put them far from you. Together they are poison emanating from your soul.

[25] Let your eyes look to the right and left and then look straight so that you may know what is about you, and use your eyelids to block out impure light.

[26] Ponder the path of your feet to avoid stumbling, thereby allowing all your ways to be established by good intentions.

[27] Turn neither to the right nor to the left to move away from good, but do well to remember to remove your foot from any evil intent.

[28] My daughter, remember, it is God's love for you, which fills His desire, that you enjoy your life, therefore know that His wisdom is there to prevent you from having unscrupulous behavior and ruining your reputation.

5

The Sensibilities of Understanding Wisdom

¹ My daughter, for you to stand on good principles, attend unto my wisdom, consider my words, and try to understand them.

² Nurture good intentions and hold on to grace and not despair. It is good to know that the words of knowledge are assuring. Be discrete and knowledgeable and bear in mind that wisdom also teaches us that life is precious.

³ My daughter, the lips of a strange man seem to drop sweetness as a honeycomb, and they can be as smooth as oil.

⁴ Some men's words are as bitter as wormwood and can sour your soul; like a sharp two-edged sword, they will cut into your spirit.

⁵ For different reasons, a strange man will travel the paths that lead toward shoal and more wickedness. Despite knowing this, he continues onward and takes hold on death, and if you go with him, there is no turning back.

⁶ My daughter, consider rather to travel the paths of life that wisdom provides and know that evil is not always visible because it can be disguised. Only by wisdom can you become familiar with wickedness, so be aware.

⁷ O ye who are loved, hear me now and henceforth depart not from the words of my mouth.

[8] Excuse yourself and be removed from her who is wicked. Stay away from the evil woman and come not nigh the door of a wicked person's house for fear of what is inside.

[9] Lest you give away your purity and honor and respect unto another, waste not your youthful years by giving them unto the cruel as a debt to sin.

❧ Desire ❦

[10] My daughter, know that slavery to fleshly lusts can start in the house of another whose needs come from lusts, and he will be filled from your lascivious acts of labor in order to satisfy them.

[11] And surely when that day comes, your soul begins to mourn and your flesh and your body are consumed.

[12] And you shall say, "Why did I hate instruction? And how much did my heart despise reproof?"

[13] A reason for your sorrow is that you did not take to heart the lessons of your teachers and you hated their instruction; you were not inclined to listen to the hints of those who instructed you!

[14] Many will say, when I was young, I was not convicted or chastised for my rebellious ways; I also ignored my own conscience because I was curious. And for all my wayward and consistent acts, which were exposed for all to see, I went on and did not change.

❧ Sexuality ❦

[15] My daughter, do not desire sex outside of marriage because they say it is OK but drink waters out of your own cistern. Running waters from your own stream is always sweeter.

[16] O my children, purity is not to be wasted and chastity is surely approved of. It is a gift most precious, for by it comes multiple blessings.

[17] Let your children be of only one husband and not gotten from many strangers, for they are an inheritance from God and they are divine.

[18] Rejoice in marriage for its benefits and be dedicated to each other and act as one. And let your womb be blessed and rejoice with his youthful embraces.

[19] Let him be to you a loving hawk, true and faithful. Also, let his ways be satisfactory to you at all times, and always be ravished with his love.

[20] And why will you, my daughter, imagine being ravished by a strange man and be fondled by or desire the embrace of a stranger?

[21] For the ways of women are also before the Lord, and He will ponder their goings entirely. And the eyes of the accuser of women are also in observance.

[22] A woman's own iniquities shall set a trap for her, and she shall be held by the cords of her sins.

[23] As a young girl is maturing and moving toward the height of her awareness, her thinking may turn to folly, then she may go astray, and her spirit shall die without knowing why.

[24] As an unbridled horse has no restraint and charges on, this is also true of a covetous spirit with selfish desires.

[25] Therefore, observe the enthusiastic woman and how she attracts attention to herself as she seeks to enslave herself to others.

6

Disaster Is Avoidable

¹ My daughter, if you make yourself responsible for your friend's debt, it may go against your own judgment if you have promised contractually to repay it.

² Know that you shall be obligated by the words of your mouth, and by your actions, you shall be bound to that stranger.

³ Do this now, my daughter. Go humbly and deliver yourself from the snare of your promises, thereby preventing more indebtedness, and work to ensure that your friend makes good on her promise.

⁴ Give no sleep to your mind or slumber to your eyelids, but work diligently to remove yourself from debt.

⁵ Work to deliver yourself with haste as a roe from the bow of the hunter and as a bird from the snare of the fowler.

⊸❧ The Folly in Idleness ❦⊷

⁶ My daughter, take a moment to glance at nature's creatures and pay attention to the ants and take note of the sluggish woman. Consider their ways and be wise.

⁷ For ants have no guide, overseer, or ruler, but they have defined their tasks.

[8] They gather their meat in the summer, and they also gather their food in the harvest. But what of the sluggard? Seasons come and go, and yet she has done no work to ensure her future.

[9] Knowing what we know of a sluggard, will she not be in need of food? How long does the sluggish woman sleep before doing labor? When will she arise and shine from her slumbering?

[10] The desire to sleep, to have more slumber is connected to the dream of only what could be, and any desire for a job to fulfill her dream is foreign to her.

[11] Many women do not know that poverty travels the world to be a companion to the lazy, and it will surely come to those who are idle. And like an armed thief, poverty will rob you.

❧ The Trouble with Folly ❧

[12] She who is naughty and she who is wicked will both go about being deceitful; they will cause much evil to come to pass by their voices.

[13] She who winks with her eyes will surely bring deception, and by waving her hand, she may cause villainy. And with her fingers, she signals cruelty because she dares not speak aloud.

[14] For her to be wicked, she must first have an insolent heart; therefore, she will devise mischief continually and will sow discord using false words.

[15] Therefore, her calamity shall come without any warning, and suddenly, she shall be broken and without any remedy.

❧ Hated ❧

[16] These six things are what the Lord hates; yea, seven are an abomination unto Him:

[17] A proud look that says "I am vain" a lying tongue that supposedly speaks the truth, hands that shed innocent blood,

¹⁸ A heart that concocts wicked imaginations, feet that are swift to commit mischief,

¹⁹ And she who is a false witness and spreads lies, someone who sows discord among women and sisters, which brings disharmony is wicked.

❧ The Wicked Spirit ❧

²⁰ My daughter, keep your father's commandments and forsake not the law of your mother.

²¹ Bind them continually upon your heart, and tie them about your neck.

²² When you awake, wisdom shall talk with you about today and when you go for a walk in the marketplace, be guided by our words because they will bring peace to an anxious soul.

²³ For my commandments are like a guide, so use them. My law will highlight your path ahead, and my reproofs carry instructions as you get involved in the ways of life.

²⁴ Wisdom will keep you from the wicked and evil man, including the flattering and seductive man.

²⁵ Lust not after his manliness in your heart; neither let him take you with his stare.

²⁶ By the influence of a whorish man, a woman's life is reduced to the cost of a loaf of bread and she will be treated like chattel, and the adulterer will also hunt for that life.

²⁷ Can a woman take fire onto her bosom and her soul not be burned? Surely all women have a delicate spirit.

²⁸ Neither can she go upon hot coals and her feet not be burned. If she is indeed lustful, her spirit is sloppy, for by her actions, she can be considered a fornicator or an adulteress.

²⁹ My daughter, she who goes unto her neighbor's husband disguised with good intentions and causes harm is guilty of much wickedness.

[30] Women do not despise a thief if she steals to satisfy her hunger, yet she is not above the law, and she will answer for it no matter the excuse.

[31] And if she be found guilty, she shall have to give all the substance of her house as payment and more until she has restored all.

[32] When a woman commits adultery with a man, she lacks understanding while giving up her dignity, and she shall carry her guilt. And she who does it destroys two souls—hers and the family.

[33] She who has a wound from dishonoring others, that is her reward, and her reproach shall not be wiped away.

[34] My daughter, jealousy can cause a woman to be enraged; therefore, she will not spare in the day of vengeance, for her anger is not easily satisfied.

[35] She will not want any ransom; neither will she rest as she is not content. And no amount of pleading or gifts will restore that which was precious regarding her dignity.

[36] Any fool who goes to meddle with a wild boar to provoke it invites injury to their flesh; so, too, will a foolish woman who provokes a man to anger.

7

Wisdom's Cautions against Sin

[1] My daughter, keep my words and lay up my commandments with you and be comforted by them.

[2] Keep my commandments and live and my law as the apple of your eye.

[3] Use them like fingers to get a handle on life and script them upon the table of your heart.

[4] Say unto wisdom, "You are as dear as my sister." And make understanding as near and dear as your favorite aunt.

⚜ Death ⚜

[5] Allow wisdom and understanding to keep you from the strange man who flatters you with his words.

[6] My daughter, as I sat at the window of my house, I looked out through my casement.

[7] And I beheld among the young ones a particular young woman acting a bit foolishly.

[8] Passing through the street near the stranger's corner, she continued on in the way that led to his house.

[9] In the twilight of the evening, in the shadows and dark of the night, she went.

[10] And behold, she met a man, dressed with the attire of a normal man who was much handsome and very subtle of heart.

[11] I noticed before that he was boisterous, full of pride, and stubborn. And within his soul, there was a jittery spirit pushing him, so he went out wandering the streets.

[12] So he went about the streets, stalking and waiting at different corners.

[13] Soon he caught her in his stare and kissed her eyes from afar and, with an impudent face, said unto her,

[14] "I prayed to God to meet someone like you, and I have presents and gifts and other trinkets that I will offer you.

[15] Diligently I came forth to meet you, and I have found you here.

[16] I have decked my couch with coverings of tapestry with sequined works and with fine linen of Egypt. I have made these things ready for you.

[17] I have perfumed my bed with myrrh, aloes, and cinnamon because I thought you would like that.

[18] Come, let us take our fill of love until the morning. Let us solace ourselves with love's embraces.

[19] For the good woman is not at home. She is gone on a long journey.

[20] She has taken much apparel and a bag of money with her, and she will come home at the day appointed."

[21] With his much fair speech, he caused her to yield. With the flattering of his lips, she succumbed to him.

[22] She went with him straightaway, as a cow goes to the slaughter and as a fool who willingly goes to the correction of the stocks.

[23] She was unwise as to what was happening till a dart seemed to strike through just below her liver and into her life's spirit, as a bird is hasty to a prize. She knew not until it was too late that a snare had been set for her life.

[24] Listen to me now, O ye children, and attend to the words of my mouth.

²⁵ Seek not nor stray into his path; let not your heart descend to surrender to him in order to seek adventure that goes against your conscientious nature.

²⁶ For he has taken that which was pure and cast it down; he has wounded and hurt many souls who were not looking for understanding as the manner of some might. Yea, many strong women have been slain by him.

²⁷ His house is known as the way to hell, because many have gone to what is known as the chambers of death where pleasure is no more.

²⁸ Because she was naive and full of desire and had no regard for her spirit, her dream was forsaken, and who she was, she is no more.

8

Wisdom's Announcement

[1] Wisdom cries out to those who wander away from the beaten path, and understanding also calls out to those who are in the city.

[2] She stands on the top of high places and in the way where paths meet.

[3] She cries at the gates of the city and to those who come in through the doors.

[4] Wisdom calls to the daughters and sons of women and men and asks that you recognize my voice.

[5] O ye simple and foolish, wisdom is needed, and for you to be capable of maintaining an understanding heart, hear my words.

[6] Listen and hear, for I will speak of excellent things. And my opening words shall be noble, for they are sweet to the ear.

[7] Out of my mouth shall come truth, and wicked words are sully and an abomination to my lips!

[8] All the words of my heart are directed toward women with a soul; there is nothing gross or perverse in them.

[9] My words are right, and they are great for her who is capable of understanding. And they will enable you to find knowledge.

[10] Receive my instruction and not silver and knowledge instead of a choice of gold; know that wisdom can make you rich.

¹¹ For wisdom is better than rubies, and all the things that you may desire are not to be compared to it. No amount of riches will deliver you from scorn.

¹² I, wisdom, dwells with prudence and discretion, but not with folly. Therefore, will you be able to find through knowledge the purpose of witty inventions?

¹³ The fear of Adonai enables us to hate evil, pride, an arrogant spirit, and any evil way. Adonai also hates a gross mouth.

¹⁴ Counsel and sound wisdom are mine. Also, I am understanding, and I give strength to your thoughts.

¹⁵ Because of me, kings and queens reign and princes and princesses make decrees regarding justice.

¹⁶ Because of me, princes and princesses rule, as do the wife and widow, and all the judges of the earth are my students.

¹⁷ I love them who love me, and those who seek me early shall find me.

¹⁸ Riches and honor are with me, yea, along with a lasting and durable inward beauty that displays righteousness.

¹⁹ The fruit of wisdom is better than fine gold and the finest silver.

²⁰ I am a leader in the ways of righteousness. In the midst of the paths of judgment, I go to provide leadership.

²¹ I seek to cause those who love me to inherit my substance; I will also help them to fill their treasure troves.

²² Adonai, the Lord of lords, possessed me before the beginning of all things, even before His works of renown.

²³ I was set up on high from everlasting, from the beginning or even before the earth ever was.

²⁴ When there were no depths, neither was there any abounding fountains of water. Therefore, I created the depths and the water to fill them, resulting in abounding fountains.

²⁵ Before the mountains and hills were settled in the waters, I was needed and was brought forth.

²⁶ Before He made the earth, the fields, the highest parts of the dust to form the world, I, wisdom, was His advisor.

²⁷ When He prepared the heavens, I was there. When He set a compass upon the face of the deep depths, I was there.

²⁸ When He established the clouds above, when He strengthened the fountains of deep waters, I was there.

²⁹ When He gave to the seas His decree, that their water should have a boundary and not go beyond it, His commandment they obeyed. And when He appointed the foundations of the earth upon which it stands, I, wisdom, was there.

³⁰ I was next to Him, as one brought up with Him, and I was His delight daily, rejoicing always before Him.

³¹ I rejoice in being in all parts of His creation, and I also delight in being there with the sons and daughters of men.

³² It is good to listen to me, O ye children, because they who speak of my ways are blessed.

³³ Listen to my instructions to be wise and refuse not to carry them out so that you can avoid bringing hurt to your whole being.

³⁴ Blessed is the woman who waits daily at the posts of my gates, listening to my words and looking for instruction.

³⁵ She who finds me finds life, and she shall obtain the favor of the Lord.

³⁶ But she who works against me will invite deception unto her own soul. All of them who hate me love death instead of life.

9

The House of Wisdom

[1] My daughter, wisdom has built her house through knowledge and hammered out her seven pillars to enable you to dwell therein.

[2] Wisdom has prepared her meats. She has made fresh wine; she has also prepared her table for guests.

[3] Wisdom has sent forth her maidens with invitations to all the women who are lacking that which satisfies. The voice of wisdom is heard crying from the highest places of the city.

[4] Whosoever is simple, let them turn in hither. As for her who wants to obtain understanding, listen because wisdom is calling.

[5] She says, "Come, eat of my bread and drink of the fresh wine that I have made."

[6] In order for you to live a good life and travel in the ways of understanding, forsake the foolish and those who have cast in their lot with the simple.

[7] If a woman reproves a scorner for mocking righteousness, she shall bring ridicule upon herself and possibly be shamed by the ungodly. She who rebukes a wicked woman will surely get herself a scarlet letter and will be mocked herself, yet the brave are rewarded.

[8] Reprove a scorner, and you may gain a friend, or she may hate you for it. Rebuke a wise woman, and she will love you for it.

[9] Give instruction to a wise woman, and she will be even wiser. Teach a just woman, and she will increase in learning.

[10] The fear of the Lord is the beginning of wisdom for a woman, and she will not be mocked by it. And the knowledge of the holy is given to her for understanding.

[11] Through wisdom's guidance, your days shall be multiplied and different types of riches shall be added to your life.

[12] If you become wise, do so for your personal gain, and your substance shall increase. But if you make a mockery of your God, you alone shall bear the offense.

◈ The Activity of Fools ◈

[13] A foolish person has no dignity and is clamorous, and the fool is a simpleton and knows nothing. Even that person's house is in disorder.

[14] Fools will sit in the door of their house for a while and then will loiter in the busy places of the city, seeking an audience.

[15] They will continue to attract passersby, calling for them to stop. The wise will not yield but will continue right on their way.

[16] Only another fool will listen and turn toward them to listen some more, and as for her who desires understanding, wisdom speaks to her.

[17] My daughter, come to understand and know that she who is enriched by stolen gems is wicked, and no matter how precious the gems are in the beginning, along with gold that is taken and admired in a secret place, they are only pleasant for a time, because they are stolen.

[18] But what she does not know is that the living dead are there in that place where merriment is had, and sultry waters are brought from that which was stolen, a place where evil and his guests are drawn into the depths of hellish appetites. They were being foolish, believing that they were deserving of those things.

[19] Therefore, her flesh and her soul shall begin to walk a path that leads to ruin by embracing the wanton pleasures of wickedness. Soon, she shall be like a cluster of grapes left to rot on the vine.

[20] Wisdom knows that the death of the soul is caused by a life of adventures and that the desire for life pleasures can cause a woman to lose all dignity and understanding.

10

A Wise Daughter Is Righteous

¹ A foolish daughter is the heaviness of her mother and is disparaging to her father, but she who is wise has a pleasant mother and a glad father.

² She who has any treasure that was obtained through wickedness profits no one, for it will not last, but righteousness delivers a prisoner from death.

³ The Lord will not suffer the soul of her who is righteous to be famished or suffer, but He shall cause the substance of the wicked woman, even the little that she has, to be consumed.

⁴ She who deals with a slack hand shall become poor, but within the hand of the diligent, there is the ability to make one rich.

⁵ She who gathers in summer is a wise daughter, but she who sleeps during harvest is a daughter who contributes to the shame of her own poverty.

⁶ Blessings will rain down upon the head of the just woman, but violence covers the body of the wicked woman like a dark cloak.

⁷ The memory of the just is blessed, but the name of the wicked shall begin to rot in the mind.

⁸ The wise in heart will receive Adonai's commandments, but a prating fool shall fall into ruin.

⁹ She who walks upright is secured by her own just actions, but she who is perverted in her ways is known to cause much sorrow.

[10] She who winks with the eye causes misery and sorrow, but she who is like a prating and proud fool shall surely fall.

[11] Within the words of a righteous woman, there is freshness for life's misgivings; they can spring up like a fountain of refreshing water. But the wicked's violent speech will be used to enrage the soul, causing the destruction of many.

[12] Hatred stirs up strife between people, but love accepts forgiveness and covers all sins that are related to trespasses or omissions.

[13] Within the lips of her who has understanding, wisdom is found, but when wanton wickedness is done without any consideration and the deed is exposed, it brings ridicule and shame.

[14] Wise women accumulate knowledge and share enough in order to keep the peace, and many are made wiser for it. But the conversation of the foolish woman is never quiet and causes destruction, and know-it-alls talk too much.

A Life of Righteousness

[15] The rich woman's wealth is gained through the labor of the poor; she who labors justly does so to avoid poverty and will labor in the rich woman's vineyards.

[16] The labor of the righteous tends to increase as life progresses; however, the fruit of the wicked is for folly and their burden is their sin.

[17] She who seeks to establish herself not just in the ways of life but also to have success will follow the instructions of wisdom, but she who refuses reproof does so because of ignorance and will err with every step.

[18] She who conceals hatred does so with lying lips, and she who utters a slander has a foolish spirit.

[19] In the multitude of words, there is an invitation to sin, but she who has knowledge of the spirit is wise and restricts her lips from too much talk.

[20] The tongue of the just is like the finest and choicest silver, yet the heart of the wicked has no worth.

[21] The lips of a righteous and wise woman will feed many, but fools die for want of knowledge.

⋙ Fear God and Live Upright ⋘

[22] The blessings of the Lord, they make a righteous woman rich, not her beauty or her ability with riches, and Adonai will not add any sorrow with it.

[23] It is a sport to a fool to do mischief, but a woman of understanding has gained her victories by using wisdom.

[24] The fear of the wicked and what an evil woman can do is disheartening even to the wicked, but the desire of the righteous shall be granted, so be patient.

[25] As the whirlwind passes on and then forgotten, so to shall the wicked who shall be no more, but the righteous are like an everlasting spring and a sound foundation that will last as long as the earth endures.

[26] Two things are unpleasant and a third is foolish: using vinegar to quench thirst and smoke in the eyes are unpleasant, and for a woman to send a sluggard on an errand is not wise, for the sluggard is sure to fail.

[27] The grace of the Lord prolongs the days of all things that He commands, and nothing is left without His instructions, but the years of the disobedient shall be few because they seek to shorten them through misdeeds.

[28] The hopes of righteous women shall be fulfilled, and a glad spirit with merriment is added to their life, but the expectation of wicked women shall perish with them.

[29] While she remains in the way of the Lord, strength is given to her who is upright, but destruction shall be to those women who are workers of iniquity.

[30] The foundations of the righteous shall never be moved since it is founded upon wisdom, and they shall forever be blessed by Adonai, but the wicked shall not inherit or be heirs with the righteous upon the earth.

[31] The mouth of the just brings forth the wisdom of the heart, but the loud voice can be like a cankerworm and the locust bug, which causes much destruction.

[32] The lips of the righteous knows what is acceptable because they speak of good tidings as they have studied much, but the mouth of the wicked spews hatred and causes much wickedness as their thoughts are jumbled.

11

The Balance in Life

[1] A false balance is an abomination to the Lord, but a just spirit is like a balanced weight, and God is delighted in them both.

[2] When pride comes, what comes next is disgrace and shame; with the modest spirit comes wisdom and great joy.

[3] She who has integrity will surely be a righteous parent, and she shall guide her children with discretion as she does with her own life, but she who is perverse and a transgressor in spirit shall destroy her children and they shall become more unruly.

[4] The riches of the just or unjust will profit little on the Day of Judgment, but righteousness is a great deliverer from death.

[5] The righteous woman who has a perfect spirit, it shall direct her, but the wicked woman shall fall due to her own wickedness.

[6] The righteousness of the upright shall deliver them, but she who is a transgressor shall be trapped by her own naughtiness.

[7] When a wicked woman dies, all her expectations shall die with her and any hope that an unjust woman placed in her will also perish.

[8] As the righteous and the wicked travel the same road, consider that there are troubles lying around like diamonds waiting to be picked up. But she who has hope in Adonai will be delivered out of danger, and she who is wicked shall inherit the danger instead.

[9] A hypocrite with her mouth destroys her neighbor, but by the knowledge of Adonai, the godly shall be delivered.

[10] When the women of the city rejoice, it is because their lives have improved due to righteousness, and when the wicked perish, there is much rejoicing.

[11] By the blessing of the upright woman, the city is exalted, but it is overthrown by the words of the wicked. However, Adonai shall silence the voices of shame.

[12] She who is void of wisdom despises her neighbor, but a woman of understanding holds her peace because she is strong in spirit.

[13] A talebearer reveals many secrets, but she who has a faithful spirit conceals the matter because she has wisdom.

[14] Where wisdom's counsel is nowhere to be found, the people fall into mischief, but in the multitude of wise women, their counsel will lead many to where there is safety.

[15] She who is surety for a stranger shall also be chained to the stranger's debt and will enslave herself and become responsible for it, but she who hates indebtedness will be a better steward of Adonai's blessings.

[16] A gracious woman retains honor and good character even in the company of others, and a strong man retains the richness of character by his labor. And together they are successful.

[17] The merciful woman does good to her own soul, but she who is cruel troubles her own flesh.

[18] The wicked are deceitful and crafty, and their reward is just. But to her who sows righteousness, she shall surely receive a righteous woman's reward, and her blessings are great.

[19] Many rewards are given toward the sustaining of life, to the righteous as a rewarded, and whoever she is who pursues evil pursues it till it causes her own death.

[20] They who are of a disobedient heart are an abomination to the Lord, but she who is upright in her ways is His delight.

[21] Women who have joined hands together to commit evil, they surely will be punished together, but the children of righteous women shall be delivered altogether, for they are joined instead with Adonai.

²² As a ring of gold in a swine's snout will serve no purpose, therefore the wicked and unrighteous woman who lacks good judgment and discretion, will surely waste her most precious gift.

²³ The desire of the righteous is to please Adonai, and that is good, but the expectation of the wicked is sure to incur His wrath.

²⁴ My daughter, she who has little but gives much, Adonai will love her spirit, and she will not be poor. But she who withholds much and exacts much is slowly losing that which she has, so be wise.

²⁵ The liberal soul shall be made fat, and she who gives to others shall be watered also herself.

²⁶ She who withholds the corn, the people shall curse her, but blessings shall be upon the head of her who is fair and sells much corn.

²⁷ She who diligently seeks good procures favor and friendships and does so with love, but she who seeks mischief need not look too far, because it shall find her instead.

²⁸ She who trusts in her riches shall fall, for they are not a true foundation, but the righteous shall flourish as a budding branch at the hint of water.

²⁹ She who troubles her own house shall inherit the storm by inviting the wind, and due to the foolishness thereof, she shall be the servant to the wise of heart for wasting her living.

³⁰ The fruit of the righteous is a tree of life, and it does not decay, and she who wins souls is wise.

³¹ Behold, O daughter, as the righteous are recompensed in the earth for their obedience, much more shall the wicked and the sinner as they are recompensed for their disobedience, because the rewards of God's Spirit are swift.

12

The Opposite of Wisdom

[1] She who loves instruction loves knowledge; she also embraces change. But she who hates criticism is brutish and does not embrace change.

[2] A good woman obtains the favor of the Lord, but a woman of wicked devices, He will condemn.

[3] A woman is not made sure or established by wickedness, thereby the root of the righteous shall not dry out.

[4] A moral man is like a jewel in the crown belonging to his wife, but he who is of low moral standards will surely bring her shame and is like rottenness in her bones.

[5] The thoughts of the righteous can be good, but the counsels of the wicked are mainly for deceit.

[6] The enabling words of the wicked teach how to lie in wait for blood, but the words of wisdom are used to strengthen justice, and they shall deliver the listeners from wickedness.

[7] The wicked are overthrown and removed, but the house of the righteous shall stand.

[8] A woman shall be commended according to her wisdom, but she who is of a perverse heart shall be despised.

[9] She who is despised and has a servant is better than she who honors herself and lacks bread, but the upright is better than them both, having neither a servant nor riches.

[10] A righteous person regards the life of all, but the tender mercies of the wicked are cruel.

[11] She who tills her land shall be satisfied with bread, but she who follows vain persons is void of understanding and shall remain hungry.

[12] The wicked woman desires to fill her life with wicked things and will do so to contend with other evil women, but the soul of the righteous woman sows hope, and that yields much fruit for herself and others to enjoy.

❧ Seeking Advice ❧

[13] The wicked woman is ensnared by the transgression of her lips, but the just woman shall come out of trouble whole.

[14] A woman shall be satisfied with good by the fruit of her conversation, and the recompense of a woman's hands shall be rendered unto her.

[15] The ways of a foolish woman is right in her own eyes, but she who hearkens unto counsel is even wiser.

[16] A fool is unashamed as she shows her body for all to see; she will also put on display anger and resentment. But a prudent woman covers her body, avoiding shame, and by having respect for others, they then will respect her in return.

[17] She who is truthful is often listened to, and her deeds are known by others to be righteous and good, but a false witness is deceitful and unjust.

[18] There are many who speak as if they were an open and bleeding wound after being pierced with a sword, but the tongue of the wise is like an ointment that brings healing.

[19] The words of truth shall be established forever, but a lying tongue and its master are but for a moment.

[20] Deceit is in the heart of them who imagine evil; however, there is much joy that comes from the words of the counselors of peace.

²¹ Therefore, no evil shall happen to her who is just, but she who is wicked shall be filled with mischief.

²² Lying lips are perverse and an abomination to the Lord, but they who deal truthfully are His delight.

²³ A prudent woman conceals knowledge and hides wisdom till needed, but the heart of the foolish proclaims foolishness as a way of life.

²⁴ The hand of the diligent soul shall bear rule, but the slothful spirit shall be under tribute.

²⁵ Heaviness that hides in the heart of a woman makes it stoop, but a good word makes her heart glad again.

²⁶ The righteous woman is more excellent than her unjust neighbor, for her ways are full of grace. But the ways of the wicked woman are seductive, and the unjust will deceive and are deceived continually.

²⁷ The slothful woman wastes most of that which she took in hunting, but the substance of a diligent woman is precious.

²⁸ Lying in the path of righteousness is the abundant life, and in the pathway thereof, there is no death.

²⁹ My daughter, there is much for you to enjoy, so spend time with like-minded people and honest friends and refrain from evil and avoid bad situations.

13

A Wise Daughter Lives Righteously

[1] A wise daughter listens and considers her father's instruction, but if she's a scorner, she will not listen to the advice of wisdom and will instead reject sound judgment.

[2] A woman shall eat well by the fruit of her mouth, but the soul of the transgressor shall be sustained by feasting on violence.

[3] She who is a careful speaker keeps her life, but she who opens wide her lips without caution shall invite destruction.

[4] The sluggard's soul dreams for and desires much, and yet she has nothing substantial, but she who is diligent shall be made fat.

[5] A righteous woman hates lying, but a wicked woman is loathsome and will surely come to be a shame to herself.

[6] Righteousness keeps her who is upright in her ways, but wickedness will overthrow the sinful woman.

[7] There is a spirit that will not enrich the life of a woman who has it, because it contains too much vanity and self-appreciation, and if a woman knows not her own true worth, neither will others. There is also a type of spirit that cannot make her who has it poor; although she has little wealth, she knows her own worth.

[8] The ransom of a woman's life is based on her riches and can invite trouble, but the poor hears no rebuke against their life for the lack thereof.

[9] The light of the righteous shines on others, and they rejoice, but the lamplight of the wicked shall be put out.

[10] My daughter, pride will bring with it a contentious and fighting spirit, but with the well-advised who practice humility, wisdom is as precious as a radiant jewel.

[11] Quick wealth gotten by vain means shall also diminish quickly, but she who gathers through labor, her stores shall increase slowly.

[12] The heart is sick when hope is deferred or crushed, but when the desire is fulfilled, it is a tree of life indeed.

[13] Whosoever despises the word of Adonai shall be destroyed not being able to fulfill or achieve any of their worldly intentions, but she who fears and commits to keeping the commandments of Adonai will consider them as being reward enough.

[14] The law of the wise woman is a fountain of life that springs from the heart, so in order for you to depart from the snares of death, sow goodness.

[15] A woman's knowledge gains her good favor, but the way of transgressors is hard and leads to their ruin.

[16] Every prudent woman deals with knowledge fit for life, but a fool lays open her folly through vain actions.

[17] My daughter, remember that a wicked messenger who lacks discretion falls into mischief as if it were a hole in the ground and is without foresight, but like a faithful ambassador who is entrusted with authority, she who reads for enjoyment has a knowledgeable spirit and is entrusted with strength and purpose.

[18] Poverty and shame shall be the reward of her who refuses instruction, but she who regards reproof shall be honored with a crown of gold.

[19] The desire of her who can accomplished much, will surely bring to the soul a sweetness, and there will be more victories, yet it is an abomination for righteous women to depart from the path of righteousness to commit evil, but not so for the foolish who strays from righteousness.

[20] She who walks with wise women shall be wise, but she who is a companion of fools shall reap the same destruction.

²¹ Wickedness and evil that are committed by sinners will be pursued with similar actions to their hurt, but to the righteous soul that commits acts of grace, and she who is righteous she will be rewarded in kind.

²² A good woman leaves an inheritance and a legacy to her children's children, and the wealth of the sinner is laid up for the just.

²³ My daughter, hard work pays a sum, thereby a farmer, through the tillage of working her field, has a good harvest and ensures her future. But for you to enjoy your harvest, consider tomorrow and do not be wasteful. But for a lack of stewardship, aa woman will lose all.

²⁴ My daughter, she who refuses to use her hand to spank her children hates to correct bad behavior and will have them to grow up being like her, but she who loves them chastens them when necessary.

²⁵ The righteous woman eats toward the satisfying of her soul, but the belly of the wicked shall want always.

²⁶ Always remember your maker during the time of sowing and reaping, and always be ready to rejoice and shout with the voice of thanksgiving, thereby giving thanks for both the first and latter rain.

14

The Ways of the Foolish Lead to Sheol

[1] Every wise woman through labor will build her house beforehand, but the foolish woman builds it only to pluck it down with her hands.

[2] She who walks in her uprightness loves and fears the Lord, but she who is perverse in her ways despises Him.

[3] My daughter, as you listen to the words of the foolish, you will come to know that they are full of nonsense, absurdities, and falsehoods. And she who shares them is full of pride. The words that come from the lips of your mother are like a lovely song, for her words are like a preservative for you to apply to your life.

[4] Where there is a clean barn and no crop, there are no oxen, but where there are oxen, there is also much work and grain. Effort, strength, and wisdom will make a good life less hard to attain.

[5] She who is a faithful witness will not lie, but a false witness will utter lies.

[6] A scorner seeks wisdom and finds it not, but knowledge is easy unto her who attempts to understand mysteries.

[7] Go from the presence of a foolish woman when you perceive that the words she shares contains neither wisdom nor knowledge.

[8] The guiding wisdom of the prudent is so that she can understand her way, but within the fool, there is a spirit of folly, deceit, and bewilderment.

[9] Fools make a mockery of justice, for they deem it to be slow. However, among the righteous, they know that justice is swift, for there is favor from God.

[10] My daughter, only you truly know your own heart's bitterness, and a friend is truly a stranger to it. Neither can she intermeddle among your feelings of joy, even though she walks the same path.

[11] A wicked woman's house shall be overthrown, but the tabernacle of the upright shall flourish.

[12] There are ways that seem right unto a woman because she is a woman, but the end thereof, if not thought upon, are the ways of death that only a woman can experience.

[13] Even in laughter, a heart can be sorrowful, and during much merrymaking, heaviness can remain.

❧ The Value of Words ❧

[14] The backslider's heart shall be filled with her own pernicious ways, and a good woman shall be satisfied from within herself.

[15] The sinner believes every word, and they are fooled into foolishness, but the prudent woman looks well into her spirit to know where her thoughts shall take her.

[16] A wise woman fears and departs from evil, but the fool is outrageous and presses forward with confidence.

[17] She who is soon angry is hasty and acts foolishly, and a woman of wicked devices is even hated among her friends.

[18] The simple inherit folly, but the prudent woman is crowned with knowledge and grace.

[19] She who is evil, her spirit shall bow before the righteous woman, and there at the gates of her who is just shall the wicked beg for help.

[20] The poor is hated even of her own neighbors because she is poor, but the rich has many friends because of their wealth, and Adonai knows them both.

²¹ She who despises her neighbor sins for a lack of wealth, but she who extends mercy to the poor, happy is she.

²² They who devise mischiefs are sure to commit errors in their life, but mercy and truth shall be granted to them who devise good.

²³ Through much labor, there is profit and security, which can be had by a woman, but to speak only of work and not labor to attend to the needs of life, a woman will live in poverty.

²⁴ The crown of wise women lies in the richness of their soul, but the souls of fools are also rich with foolishness.

²⁵ A true witness delivers souls, but a deceitful witness speaks lies and causes shame.

⊸❧ The Lord ❧⊷

²⁶ Having the fear of the Lord, a parent will take charge of her family, having a strong and steady confidence, and all of Adonai's children shall have a place of refuge.

²⁷ Having the fear of the Lord is to be compared to a fountain of life-giving water to keep the thirsty soul from the snares of death.

²⁸ By the support of a multitude of people, the queen is honored, and substantial gifts are added to enable her to uphold the graces of God. Therefore, a princess should know that in giving in to the whims of the just and the unjust alike will cause her own destruction.

²⁹ She who is slow to judgment understands the rule of law, but she who has a hasty spirit promotes folly and is not supported.

³⁰ A sound heart is good and brings life to the flesh, and she who envies others invites ruin, which brings rottenness to her bones, causing her spirit to mourn.

³¹ She who oppresses the poor reproaches her Maker, but she who honors Adonai bestows mercy on the poor.

³² My daughter, a queen who is wicked will be rejected because of her wickedness, and the righteous becomes hopeful in her death.

[33] Wisdom rests in the heart of her who has understanding, but stupidity, which does not rest, is revealed and made known in the midst of fools as well as the wise.

[34] Righteousness exalts a nation and makes it great in the eyes of the just and unjust alike, but sin is a reproach to any people and will invite more corruption from within and without.

[35] The queen's favor is hastened toward a wise servant, but her support is not given to someone who causes her shame.

15

A Good Speech

¹ A woman's knows that a soft answer turns away wrath, and any grievous words spoken to insult another woman either in jesting or anger shall stir up anger.

² The tongue of the wise uses knowledge aright, but the mouth of fools pour out foolishness.

³ The eyes of the Lord looks into and around all things; He beholds the evil and the good in action.

⁴ A wholesome tongue is refreshing, and like a drink of water, it gives life to the receiver. But willful perverse words will cause a breach in the spirit.

⁵ A fool despises her father's instruction, resulting in mockery, but she who accepts his criticism is prudent, and it shows in her character.

⁶ In the house of the righteous, much of life's treasure is diverse, but within the house of the wicked those who devise wicked devices, their revenue brings trouble.

⁷ The lips of the wise disperse knowledge, but the foolish heart is uncooperative and denies wisdom a place for instruction.

⁸ My daughter, the sacrifice of the wicked is selfish and an abomination to the Lord, but the prayer and the sacrifice of the upright is His delight.

⁹ The ways of the wicked is an abomination unto the Lord, but He loves to acquaint Himself with her who follows after righteousness.

¹⁰ My daughter, giving correction to the wicked can be a burden, and she who hates reproof shall have a short existence, for she desires to go from the right way and instead move toward intermingling with sin.

¹¹ The Lord sees all things that exist in the universe, for they are always in His view. How much more are the hearts of the children of women?

❖ Lifting of Spirits ❖

¹² Reprove not a scorner for she will not love you for it; neither will she go unto the wise women for understanding.

¹³ A merry heart makes a cheerful countenance, and it is shown in a smile on the face. And a wise spirit can be broken if the heart begins to fill with sorrow.

¹⁴ The heart of her who has understanding seeks knowledge, but the mouth of fools spews out foolishness.

¹⁵ She who is always anxious is afflicted with indifference; therefore, she will be susceptive to evil daily. But she who is of a merry heart and is content shall always have a continual feast.

¹⁶ A woman who has the fear of the Lord is made all the better by it, for she will value what she has more than any treasure that is considered to have greater value.

¹⁷ A simple dried salad is better if served where there is love, more so than a succulent meal of dainty and prepared meats where there is disdain.

¹⁸ A wrathful woman stirs up strife, but she who is slow to anger works against strife.

¹⁹ To travel through a field of thorns is hard, and so is labor to a slothful woman, but the path of the righteous woman is paved and made easy by her labor.

²⁰ A wise daughter makes a glad father, but a foolish woman despises even her mother's righteousness.

²¹ Folly and ignorance are greeted with enthusiasm by her who is destitute of wisdom, but a woman of understanding walks uprightly and is joyful for having wisdom as her companion.

²² Without counsel, a woman with a purpose can be disappointed thereby, but she who knows that having a multitude of counselors is needed, afterward she can rejoice that her purpose can be established.

²³ A woman has joy of heart by the answer of her mouth, and a word spoken in due season can be like a fresh fragrance. How good it is!

²⁴ The ways of life are given from above in order to lead the wise so that she may depart from hell beneath.

²⁵ The Lord will destroy the house of the proud from without and will establish the border of the widow from within.

²⁶ The thoughts of the wicked are an abomination to the Lord, but the words of the pure are like pleasant vapors.

²⁷ She who is greedy for filthy lucre will be ridiculed; it will surely trouble her own house. But she who hates illegal gifts shall have peace.

²⁸ The heart of the righteous woman studies to provide an answer, but the mouth of the wicked woman does not hesitate to pour out evil sayings.

²⁹ The Lord is far from the wicked and allows them freedom to choose their own path through the rejection of Him, but He hears the prayer of the righteous and aids them in making decisions.

³⁰ Wisdom can cause the eyes of her who has it to light up and her face to rejoice, causing her heart to swell, and a good report will surely make her bones fat. Therefore, an intelligent woman shall be made exceptional.

³¹ She who listens to the reproof of life is found among wise friends and is considered worthy of outward praise, unlike the perverse, for their ways are unruly and not deserving of such friends.

³² She who refuses instruction despises her own soul, but she whose soul is encouraged to listen to reproof obtains and keeps understanding.

³³ The instruction of wisdom is gained after one fears the Lord, and humility comes before honor is bestowed.

³⁴ My daughter, always remember the tenets of God and look to be guided by His spirit instead of your own intuition. Consequently, in order for you to succeed, be ready to embrace change.

16

The Blessings of Wisdom

¹ The preparations of the heart in a woman and the answer of her tongue are from the Lord.

² All the ways of a woman are clean in her own eyes, for she cannot fully comprehend her own faults, but the Lord weighs more than just her spirit's intentions.

³ My daughter, if you would commit your works unto the Lord, your thoughts, coupled with good intentions, shall be established.

⁴ The Lord has made all things for Himself. Yea, even the wicked one for the day of evil. And you, O my children, He made to dwell in His presence.

⁵ Everyone who is overtly proud in heart is conceited; they are an abomination to the Lord. As one heart and like two hands joined, they all will be punished as one.

⁶ Through mercy and by your own truthful spirit, iniquity is purged from your soul. Therefore, if a woman were to have the fear of the Lord, she can depart from evil.

⁷ When a woman's ways please the Lord, He makes even her enemies to be at peace with her, and blessings are assured.

⁸ With a little wealth, a woman can do much if she is a righteous steward, yet she who has great revenues without wisdom does little except to waste it.

⁹ A woman's heart directs her way, because the Lord devises her steps.

⋙❀ Life's Not Immune to Waste ❀⋘

¹⁰ A divine sentence comes forth from the mouth of the queen; her voice transgresses not the judgment of righteousness.

¹¹ A just weight and balance are of Adonai's design; all the proper weights of the bag are His and are given to us for His work.

¹² It is an abomination for queens to commit wickedness from the throne, because the throne is established by righteousness and is a measure by which to meet out the justice of God.

¹³ A woman who speaks words of wisdom can be the delight of any queen, and they love her, for her speech is just and right.

¹⁴ The wrath of a queen, although tempered, can be like messengers of death, but a wise woman may pacify her wrath with fair speech.

¹⁵ In the light of the queen's countenance is warmth, and her favor upon you is like a cloud providing the latter rain.

¹⁶ How much better is it to get wisdom than gold or silver? Through the obtaining of wisdom, there is much understanding, which is better than untarnished silver or unrefined gold! My daughter, true wisdom is incorruptible.

¹⁷ To depart from the evil way, know that the highway of the just lies there before you. Therefore, if a woman finds and travels it, she is wise, and she is sure to preserve her soul.

¹⁸ Selfish pride and an insulting spiritual attitude will lead to a fall from grace, resulting in destruction, and not having understanding is the reason.

¹⁹ Better it is to be of a humble spirit with a lowly heart and a piece of gold than to unjustly divide great spoil among the proud.

²⁰ She who handles a matter wisely shall find good, and the woman who trusts in the Lord, happy is she.

[21] She who is wise of heart shall be called prudent; her words do inspire, and they are sweet. Therefore, she shall be mimicked by the learned but mocked by the unjust.

[22] Understanding is a wellspring of life unto her who has it, but the instruction of fools leads only to folly.

[23] The mind directs the heart of a woman through many mistakes, and it teaches her mouth words. And with learning added to her lips, she speaks with perception and discretion. And by her actions, she is thought of as being wise.

[24] The pleasing and pleasant words of a woman or a man are like a honeycomb, sweet to the soul and healthy for a person's well-being.

[25] She who is not aided in decision-making and not directed while young toward a certain path, any path is good because it seems right, but at the end thereof, she knows not what is there unless it is shown to her by wisdom.

[26] She who labors, labors to ensure for herself a quality of life that will be satisfying to both body and soul, for her being craves it of her, but she who refuses to do that which is necessary will surely miss out on opportunities that are presented to her.

[27] An ungodly woman digs up evil, and within her lips, there is a burning fire.

[28] A froward woman sows strife, and a whisperer speaks with the intention to separate chief friends.

[29] My daughter, know that a seducing and unjust woman entices her neighbor to commit sin and leads her into the violent way, and that is not good.

[30] She who shuts her eyes to dream in order to devise froward things can, by simply moving her lips, signal others to bring evil to pass.

[31] The silver hair of a woman is a crown of glory, if she be known to be in the way of righteousness. For it is more than a covering; it is a light to wayward.

[32] My daughter, take notice of her who is slow to anger, for she is sure to stand among the mighty, and she who controls her spirit is someone who can rule a city.

[33] My daughter, when seeking a position, know that the stones cast by wise women into the bowl and drawing out a stone for the answer is wise, but also know that the whole disposing of the process is the Lord's doing, so pray.

17

Wisdom Knocks on the Mind

¹ How much better is it to have a meal consisting of dry herbs and quietness to aid digestion therewith than a house full of dainty sacrifices with strife?

² She who is a wise servant shall have rule over a daughter who causes shame; therefore, she shall have a portion of the child's inheritance for her service.

³ The fining pot is for trying silver, and the furnace is for proving gold. It is also good that the Lord tries the hearts of all women and men from His throne.

⁴ A wicked doer's advice is deceitful, as her lips speaks falsely. And she who is a liar desires that others give their attention to a lying tongue; only another wicked person listens.

⁵ When the wicked mocks the poor, they reproach her Maker, and she who is glad at calamities shall not go unpunished.

⁶ The glory that results from guiding a child in life is due to their mother and father's wisdom, and their children's children is the crown on the head of the elderly.

⁷ A fool's speech sounds excellent, but listen closely and know folly. So, too, does the lying lips of a princess reflects her intentions.

⁸ An unsolicited gift is like a precious stone in the eyes of her who has it; therefore, it shall bring prosperity and blessings to her.

[9] A wise woman will overlook a transgression because of love, but she who exposes a matter will do so to forsake any friendships and will cause riffs in relationships.

[10] A reproof for an error in judgment will surely enter into the mind of a wise woman, but to a silly fool, reproof will not matter, because a silly fool will fall into the same hole continuously.

[11] A contentious, evil woman creates rebellion by the fire of descent; therefore, a cruel messenger shall be sent against her.

[12] A wise woman whose passion is peace will not venture into the path of a woman who has given in to a type of anger that is similar to a bear who has lost her cubs, but she who is foolish cares not and will intermeddle with her.

[13] She whose intent is to reward evil for good, evil shall return and wait for her, and it shall not depart from her house.

[14] The beginning of strife is similar to someone pouring out water in times of drought; therefore, leave off contention before it can be intermeddled with.

[15] My daughter, if a woman justifies the wicked and condemns the just and excuses all unrighteousness, she is an abomination to the Lord.

[16] My daughter, God has placed wisdom within the reach of women, and it is not pricey. Even the wicked and foolish women can purchase it, but the slothful seem to have no heartfelt desire for it.

❧ Be Sure of Yourself ❧

[17] A friend's love is eternal and does not diminish, and a sister is birthed for adversity. For such is her way, and they are both made better for it.

[18] A woman void of understanding will clasped hands and then go ahead with an agreement to bind her life with a friend. When her friend is unable to pay, she then becomes, in time, responsible, and with it comes the possibility of bringing ruin to herself.

¹⁹ She who loves strife is boastful and a transgressor, thereby inviting trouble, and by exalting her own gate, she looks to cause arguments and will ensure her own destruction.

²⁰ She who has a false heart, good can elude her, and any attempt to capture it is futile. And she who has a perverse tongue falls into mischief.

²¹ She who begets a fool by teaching folly, she will surely bring regret and sorrow to her door. And the father of a foolish daughter has no joy, for she belongs to her mother.

²² All spiritual good causes merriment to the heart like a medicine, but a brittle spirit is soon to be broken like dried bones.

²³ A wicked woman who takes a gift into her bosom and does so to pervert the ways of justice will do so at a great cost.

²⁴ Wisdom is before all things, and it provides great vision to women who have understanding. But the vision of a fool is short-sided, and those who will not venture to gaze toward the end of important matters will travel a dark path, not truly knowing the end thereof.

²⁵ A grieving father has a fool for a daughter, and to the mother who bore her, she is like a bitter fruit.

²⁶ It is not good to stand against her who is just and forthright, nor is it wise to strike a princess for instituting equity to the poor.

²⁷ She who has knowledge speaks wisely and spares her words, and a woman of understanding has an excellent spirit.

²⁸ She who is wise knows when to speak and will be considered knowledgeable and will always listen to the whole matter, but a fool will utter her heart and will provide no solution. Therefore, she who does not speak out of turn or without knowledge is esteemed a woman of understanding.

²⁹ My daughter, too much wine can dull the sensibilities of a woman causing rude behavior, but fools act foolishly and will do so without a cup in their hand, and both are without merit.

18

How Important Are Your Words?

[1] Through desire, a woman, having separated herself from seeking and intermeddling with soulish pleasures and certain friendships, does so with the intent to seek wisdom.

[2] To a foolish woman, her own understanding is as foreign as a stranger's glance, yet her delights are simple and defined by the feeling in her heart. She may then uncover them and will speak with an unbridled tongue.

[3] When the wicked comes, they bring with them contempt, disrespect, ignominy, nakedness, and reproach, but the righteous seeks redemption from shame.

[4] My daughter, let your mind be as calm as deep waters, and like a wellspring that exits into a flowing brook guiding a flower over the rocks, let Adonai's words guide you through life.

[5] To attempt to overthrow the righteous in judgment by accepting a well-known person over the unknown in judgment is not wise, and it is an abomination in the sight of Adonai.

[6] A fool's words will lead her to enter into contention with friends and others, for her mouth calls for adversity to happen.

[7] If a woman has a fool's mouth, her own words will cause her to drink and eat her own destruction, then shall her soul and will be ensnared by her appetites.

[8] The words of a busybody causes wounds that do not heal, for they shall find their way down into the innermost parts of the belly.

❧ High-Mindedness ❧

[9] She who is also slothful in her work has a mediocre spirit and is a sister to her who is a great waster.

[10] The name of the Lord God is a strong tower; the righteous woman runs into it and finds shelter and is safe.

[11] The rich woman's conceitedness will lead her to believe that her wealth provides her with some shelter as a walled city; she even thinks it will protect her from God.

[12] A woman's haughty spirit will lead her forward into the grasp of destruction. In order for her to avoid failure, it is paramount that she be of a humble spirit.

[13] She who interrupts others to speak words without having a reason to do so but simply to speak out of turn is a cause for foolishness; she then brings shame unto herself and those who hear her.

[14] A woman who derives help from the Lord's Spirit can sustain her dignity and be able to obtain healing for her infirmities, but a strong woman who has a wounded spirit and is without any guidance being alone with grief, even she cannot bear it alone.

[15] The heart of the prudent acquires knowledge by seeking it, and knowledge is tested by the ear.

[16] A woman's gift, like a nurturing spirit, will make room for her, and it will bring her before great women of understanding.

[17] She who is first in her own cause seems justified in finding a resolution, but when her neighbor comes and she is tried, her cause is then in question.

[18] She who is posted to a position of leadership has gotten and received it by lot, and with such confidence, the contentions of the mighty are ceased.

[19] A sister offended is harder to be won than a strong city. Because of her contentious spirit, she can be like the bulwarks of a castle, hard to be won over.

[20] My daughter, as your wisdom increases, your belly shall be filled by the fruit of your lips, and you shall be satisfied.

[21] Death and life are in the power of the tongue. And they who love a good life have a powerful voice and shall eat the fruit thereof, but they who speak words of mourning, their spirit is versed in bewilderment and the words they profess are weak and their life's work is stagnant.

[22] She who looks at a man through the spiritual eyes of faith will see him working in the field, and if she also desires a husband, she will find a good thing and obtain the favor of the Lord. But she who looks for him and finds him in a dream does not know to look for trouble.

[23] The poor, for a lack of riches, begs for justice; but the rich, because they are prosperous, will have no regard for the poor and will treat them not as equals and will answer them rudely.

[24] A woman who desires and has friends does so by showing that she has the spirit of Adonai, who is also friendly, and He is a friend who sticks closer than a sister.

[25] My daughter, Adonai sees that which your soul desires and seeks after. Also know that your desires may cause you to do whatever it takes to fulfill them; therefore, always use understanding so that you may choose wisely.

19

Listen and Learn

¹ My daughter, walk with integrity and be content, and you shall have a peaceful existence. Without which, your spirit is sure to be restless, and you may be considered as a fool.

² Also, for your soul to be without knowledge, it is not good; therefore, she who is wanton and has a hasty spirit shall run into ill repute and sin with strangers.

³ The foolishness of a woman will pervert her ways, but when the expected end is not according to her liking, she then blames the Lord.

⁴ My daughter, wealth will obtain for you many friends and things, but the poor are separated from their neighbor for the lack thereof. But she who is a servant of Adonai will not be lacking for opportunities to be rich.

⁵ A false witness shall not escape punishment, when justice is due, neither shall she who speaks lies escape judgment.

⁶ Many will entreat the favor of the princess for earthy gain and status, and every woman wants to be a friend to her in order to obtain that gift.

⁷ All the sisters of the poor do hate her because she is in need, and they are made poor for it. How much more do her friends go far from her? Even though she pursues them with words of friendship, yet they depart, leaving her with her desires unfulfilled.

[8] She who gets wisdom loves her own soul, and she who has understanding is nurtured and shall find good in self and in others.

[9] A false witness is surely to be punished, and she who speaks lies shall be ruined by them.

[10] Life's delicacies and delights are not seemly for a fool, much less is it justified for a servant to have the rule over a princess, for it is folly.

[11] The discretion of a woman whose breathing is quick causes her to defer her anger, and it is her spirit that will allow her to pass over a transgression.

[12] The queen's wrath is like the roaring of a lioness because of its hunger, but her favor is like manna from God, destined for the satisfaction of many.

[13] A foolish daughter is the calamity of her mother and a shame to her father, and she who is like an open roof with a continuous drip will easily agitate her husband.

[14] Much richness is to be gained from the mother's spiritual insight, and a wise and prudent husband is from the Lord.

[15] She who is slothful does so easily find comfort in sleeping, and an idle soul shall suffer hunger for lack of effort.

[16] She who keeps the commandments of Adonai keeps her own soul, but she who despises to walk in His ways shall die.

[17] She who has pity upon the poor and shares her substance does so believing that she is giving unto God, and that which she has shared with others. God will in return provide much to her!

[18] Chasten your daughter swiftly as she grows and hope for good behavior, and let not your soul spare specific corrections, for her crying is short-lived.

❖ Livelihood ❖

[19] She who has delivered a woman or friend who has no self-control has done it many, many times, and yet you must do it yet again. Surely a woman having great anger will eventually suffer punishment.

²⁰ She who hears counsel and receives instruction shall gain wisdom enough that she may have something to reap in her latter endings.

²¹ There are many devices in a woman's heart, and that which should be paramount is the counsel of the Lord.

²² As a woman's inward kindness is shown to be delightful, it will surely be desired by men, for she goes about sharing what little she has. Whether poor or rich, a lying woman has no kindness; therefore, she is neither desirable nor delightful.

²³ The fear of the Lord is intended to bring good into a woman's life, and she who has it shall abide satisfied and shall not be visited with evil.

²⁴ A slothful woman hides her hand in her bosom and will not so much as bring it to her mouth; she will instead wait to be fed at a great cost to herself.

²⁵ My daughter, the rebuking of a scorner may give guidance to the simple, and they who have understanding will gain more knowledge.

²⁶ She who wastes her father's words and chases away her mother is a daughter who causes shame and brings disgrace and reproach to her family.

²⁷ Cease, my daughter, and do not listen to words that causes you to err from the instruction of knowledge.

²⁸ In secret, she who is ungodly shows her disgust even for her own unjust actions, yet she will continue to commit more atrocities. Therefore, she shall be devoured from within by her own iniquitous nature.

²⁹ For those who cannot contain their foolishness, judgments will be written and made ready and prepared for them, along with shackles, restraints, and punishments, which are justified.

³⁰ She who tears at another's soul, desiring to expose its secrets and acts of sin, will also expose her own diseases, for her cruelties and lusts are just as many.

20

Spiritual Confusion

¹ Women are mocked after drinking too much wine and strong drink. Lacking understanding, they relent to being unbridled and, without restraint, becoming enraged.

² The rage of a queen is as frightful as the roaring of a lioness; it behooves you to know that whosoever she is who goes about to provoke her to anger works against her own soul. And it is the same with Adonai. Do not incur His wrath.

³ For a woman to cease from strife, that can be a crowning moment, and she gives honor to her own soul. But she who is very foolish will continue to meddle.

⁴ The sluggard will not sow any seed and will blame it on the weather; therefore, she shall begin to beg after the harvest because of her lack of effort.

⁵ Counsel that lies in the heart of a good woman is like a deep well full of water, but a woman of understanding will draw it out with a rope and a bucket.

⁶ Most women will proclaim to everyone her own trustworthiness, but a faithful woman is much sought after!

⁷ The just woman who walks upright, her integrity precedes her, and her many generations are also blessed by Adonai.

⁸ A queen who sits upon the throne of judgment is capable and shall scatter all evil with her glare.

[9] Can a woman truly say "I have made my heart clean, and I am made pure from my sin of adultery" and that by her own efforts?

[10] Diverse weights and diverse measures, if believed to be equal but are not, are an abomination to the Lord, for they are false. How much more is the unbalanced soul teetering on injustice?

[11] My daughter, by observing your children, you can know them and their doings, whether their works be pure or whether they are wicked, but know that when their actions calls unto you for correction, do not hesitate.

⤳ Spiritual Knowledge ⤳

[12] The hearing ear and the seeing eye, the Lord did make both of them to make us wise.

[13] My daughter, as you look upon the wheat field and find it is harvest time, you can truly say, "I love the industrious life, for I have no interest in becoming poor." And as you open wide your eyes, you know you shall be satisfied with bread.

[14] "It is not worth it. It is not worth it," says the buyer when buying goods. But when she is gone on her way, she then boasts of her dealings, believing that she can bargain.

[15] Much is to be gained by having gold and a multitude of silver. To a fool, they are but rocks to be wasted, but to a knowledgeable woman, the gold that she gets from the lips of a wise woman is like a good medicine.

[16] My daughter, give not your property to a stranger to hold as an agreement for payment for a loan because that person will take it in exchange, and neither should you make a loan to another. Instead, you take a pledge of her for repayment of the loan given.

[17] For an ungodly woman who goes about to obtain bread by deceitful practices, to her it is sweet, but afterward, her mouth shall be filled with gravel and her soul is not nourished.

[18] Every honorable purpose is established by wise counsel, and only with good advice, make war.

[19] She who goes about as a talebearer reveals secrets; beware and do not intermingle with her who flatters with her lips, feigning friendship, so that she may become your ally.

[20] She who curses her father or her mother shall have her lamp put out and become ambiguous and will dwell in obscure darkness.

[21] She whose inheritance is received in part or in full with haste is wasteful, for the end thereof shall not be blessed for a lack of wisdom.

[22] She who says "I will repay the works of evil" is not wise. Instead, wait on the Lord, for He shall rescue you from destruction.

[23] She who is a deceiver is like a bag of false balances. Her ways are uneven and not good, and she stands before Adonai as an abomination.

[24] A spiritual woman's travels are guided by the Lord, but she who is carnal lacks guidance and will not understand why the road she travels through life is so hard, is it because she lacks direction.

[25] It is a snare to the woman who speaks swiftly to that which is holy, and after her vow goes about, to then make inquiry is not wise. So make no unnecessary vows, and you will not have to be beholden to God or anyone else.

[26] A wise queen scatters the wicked as though they were winnow, and like wheat in the threshing house under the wheel, she declares and brings judgments over them.

[27] The body of a woman is similar to that of a man in that they contain the light of the Lord, and by that light, her spirit can search all the inward parts of the belly.

[28] Grace and truth preserves the queen and her authority, and her throne is upheld because of the mercy bestowed by righteousness.

[29] The glory of young women is their strength of beauty and grace of character with a pure heart. And the beauty of a saintly woman's gray hair with friends around is like a crown, and she will be admired.

[30] A godly woman, like the blueness around a wound cleanses away disease, who seeks righteous and commits just actions will cleanse away evil from her soul.

[31] She who seeks wickedness is sure to be preyed upon.

21

The Lord Gives Direction

[1] The queen's heart is in the hand of the Lord. As the rivers of water are directed by mountain paths, Adonai guides her heart in good directions according to His will.

[2] A woman's ways are right in her own eyes, but the Lord considers her heart's true intentions.

[3] For a queen to have good judgment and a heart that is guided toward providing justice is more acceptable to the Lord than any of her personal sacrifices.

[4] A scornful look and a vain heart are derived from the inner workings of the soul, and they are sinful.

[5] My daughter, she who plans and works diligently will be rewarded in time; they who are not patient and gives in to haste will surely come to ruin.

[6] If a woman were to obtain a treasure by lying in order to gain an advantage, like a creeping fox, she will be found out.

[7] The foolish actions of the wicked shall destroy them, because they reject the notion of good judgment.

[8] She whose actions are strange can become known as froward, but as for the pure, her work is commendable.

Be Prepared

⁹ It is better for a woman to dwell in a secluded place, away from a man who has an aggressive spirit, because in a wide house, there is no running room.

¹⁰ The soul of the wicked desires evil and will not find the company of a righteous woman comforting.

¹¹ When the scorner is punished, the simple are observant and made wise, and when a woman who is wise is instructed, she receives more wisdom.

¹² The righteous woman notices that God will eventually overthrow the wicked and thoughtfully considers it.

¹³ Whosoever stops her ears at the cry of the poor, she also shall cry, but none will answer, for she also shall not be heard.

¹⁴ A secret bribe will pacify the anger of the wicked; therefore, the greater the anger, the greater the gift must be.

¹⁵ It is of great joy to the just to witness fair judgment, yet there is no joy to the spirit to punish the workers of iniquity.

¹⁶ The woman who wanders out of the way of understanding, her wanderings will surely lead her into the congregation of the dead.

¹⁷ She who loves the pleasures of life without objectivity shall be pitied for lacking good sense, and she shall be made poor for the lack thereof. And she who loves wine and trinkets is lonely and desires friends and will not be made rich in either.

¹⁸ The wicked shall be like a ransom for the righteous, along with the transgressor who will instead be given up for the upright.

¹⁹ It is better for a woman to dwell in the wilderness than with a contentious and angry man in a house where there are no barriers.

²⁰ In the dwelling of the wise, there is much treasure with oil that was earned by fair labor, and those who see it desire the same. But she who is foolish, her vanity will be the cause of her poverty, for she wastes her treasure on pleasures.

²¹ She who follows after righteousness and mercy finds a life that is filled with righteousness and honor, having received them from the Lord.

²² My daughter, know that by the strength of wisdom and good character, a wise woman can overcome or climb any obstacle, because her spirit is not dismayed, for she has the courage of a faith warrior.

✤ The Boundaries of Life ✤

²³ Whosoever keeps her mouth and her tongue keeps her soul from troubles.

²⁴ She who is a proud and haughty scorner shall be known by the name disrespectful, for her tendency is to go beyond the boundaries of life and over and into spaces that contain misgivings, not giving heed to her conscientious spirit.

²⁵ She who is lazy does nothing; her only desire is to fulfill her fleshly cravings. And for her spirit to be satisfied with sleep and because her hands refuse to do labor, she then resorts to riotous living, thereby causing injury to her soul.

²⁶ Therefore, she will work all day long to simply satisfy her cravings and desires and nothing more, but the righteous, being content with a simple life and having satisfied themselves through much awareness, sher also loves to give out to others from her treasures chest and spares not.

²⁷ The actions of a wicked spirit that offers sacrifices in service to the Lord is hypocritical and does not serve God, nor does she do justice to her soul, for her thoughts are appalling.

²⁸ In judgment, a false witness shall bring ruin to her soul for a lack of prudence, but the woman who hears and speaks consistently with prudence is pure, knowing God's judgment.

²⁹ A woman who goes out of the way to commit wickedness does so with a hardened heart and a look of determination on her face. Now concerning the upright who walk with the spirit, their countenance does show the glory of their maker on their forehead.

³⁰ My daughter, no matter how much wisdom or understanding or counsel or reasoning that you obtain by studying or observing or

learning, it will not stand against the Lord your God in judgment of yourself.

[31] She who is prepared to match and stand against the rigors of life is brave and shows majesty, but it is only by the Lord's Spirit that safety is achieved.

22

Having Integrity

[1] A caring woman with a good name and loving favor is better than an established reputation made up of silver and gold.

[2] The rich and poor meet together around His throne, for the Lord is the maker of them all.

[3] A prudent woman foresees the evil and hides herself, but the simple will continue onward and are punished.

[4] By humility and with fear of the Lord, riches and honor with a good quality of life can be achieved.

[5] Thorns and snares lay in the way of the froward, for they desire wayward activities. But she who has a great regard for life and liberty shall not stray far from the path of glory and will not stray unto the path of the wicked.

[6] My daughter, show yourself as a fine example in the sight of your children. As a guide who leads others through the forest, lead your children in such a way that when they mature, their paths will lead them to God.

[7] The rich rule over the poor, for they lack riches; thereby they will become a servant to the lender for the same reason.

[8] She who sows iniquity shall reap wickedness, and that is a cause for pain. Therefore, her anger shall be turned upon herself.

[9] She who is blessed with goods and has a bountiful eye shall be called blessed, for she gives of her bread to the poor.

¹⁰ Cast out the foreign tongue of a scorner, thereby snuffing out contention. Yea, all strife and reproach against others shall cease.

¹¹ She who is of a pure heart is known by her name and is much loved, and she is graced by the lips of others. And the queen shall hear and be her friend.

¹² The eyes of the Lord see and preserve the knowledgeable, and Adonai will surely overthrow the words of the transgressor.

¹³ The slothful woman's reason for her laziness is, "There is a lion lurking about. I shall be slain in the streets."

¹⁴ The deceitful words of a stranger are truly a quagmire; therefore, she who is disobedient to God shall fall therein.

¹⁵ Foolishness seeks to bind itself upon the heart of a child, but the gloved hand of correction upon the buttocks shall drive it far from them.

¹⁶ She who oppresses the poor to increase her riches and she who gives only to the rich, they shall surely come to want that which brings meaning to life, which is self-worth.

❧ Wise Words Are Received ❧

¹⁷ My daughter, hear the words of your father. Bow down your ear and happily, or by chance, apply knowledge to your heart and understand the words of your mother, for she is perceptive.

¹⁸ How sweet and pleasant it would be if you keep words of wisdom echoing within you; thereby your words shall be fitting coming from your lips and easy upon the ear.

¹⁹ I have made known to you this day, even to you, for you to place your trust in the Lord.

²⁰ Wisdom has a legacy on how to obtain prosperity, and for you to obtain excellent things through counsel and knowledge, practice having fortitude.

²¹ The might of wisdom is to make you know the certainty of the words of truth, that you may answer by the words of truth those who inquire of you.

²² She who is in authority should not rob the poor because they are poor, nor should she oppose the afflicted in the place of judgment.

²³ For Adonai will plead their cause and spoil the conscience of those who defraud them and others.

²⁴ Make no friendship with an angry woman lest she angers you, and with a furious woman, you should not go because you also can become enraged.

²⁵ If you go about to learn their ways, your soul shall ensnare itself, and you may be bound by the deeds of wickedness.

²⁶ My daughter, ensure that you do not become indebted with another or someone who is responsible for the another's debt. Why should you enslave yourself?

²⁷ Therefore, if you have nothing to give as payment, do not ask why when they come to take away your bed from under you.

²⁸ Women do not remove the ancient landmarks that other women have set for themselves by using deceit, for they have justly obtained it. Know that the Lord is always watching.

²⁹ She who is diligent in her business, the queen shall hear and desire her wisdom and will bring her within the midst of diligent women like herself.

23

Be Careful Around Others

[1] When you sit at the table to eat with a woman who is a ruler, consider diligently what is before you, for your actions shall reflect back at you, and your appetite will speak for you.

[2] Therefore, consider to put a knife to your throat if you be a woman who likes to greatly indulge her appetite for the taste of dainty meats. Be aware and wait until you are at home, lest your host think evil of you.

[3] Never desire to be like her as she may be pretentious. As for her true delicacies, they may be used to deceive you. Therefore, she shall disguise her true intentions so that she may have a reason to accuse you.

[4] She who is good will work to be rich and will use her own wisdom and will work not to defraud.

❧ That which deceives ❧

[5] Will you set your eyes upon that which is vain and covet it? For riches certainly do diminish and are gone. They make themselves wings, as if they were a bird and fly away.

[6] Eat not the bread of her who has a deceiving look; neither desire her deceptive ways.

[7] "Eat and drink," she says to you. But in her heart, she thinks about sharing ever so little, because she is selfish, and what she does, she does begrudgingly, thinking of the cost of the meal.

[8] Therefore, the morsel that you have eaten shall be vomited because you know the morsel is more important than you, and your sweet words will have been wasted for the knowledge that your host deceived you.

[9] She who is a fool will put no value on your speech, for her ears are like that of a statue, they hear not.

[10] Remove not the boundaries set by those who were before us, and take not that which belongs to the fatherless, for they are there for the protection of all our souls.

[11] Know, therefore, that their redeemer is mighty when they are weak; He shall take up their cause against you.

[12] She who applies her heart by giving it instructions and lending her ears to the words of knowledge is wise.

[13] Withhold not the correction from the child, for if you continually put upon her the words of instruction, she shall not die.

[14] Therefore, instruct her with words of wisdom from above, and you shall deliver her soul from hell below.

[15] My daughter, if your heart be wise, my heart shall also rejoice, and I will be comforted.

[16] Yea, my belly shall also rejoice with laughter when your lips speak of right things.

[17] Let not your heart envy sinners, for there is nothing to be gained. But if it is prosperity that you seek, then fear the Lord all day long, and He will give it you.

[18] Your expectation shall not be cut off suddenly, because with God, there is a good ending.

[19] My daughter, listen and be wise and allow my words to guide your heart in the ways of life.

[20] Be not found among wine tasters for sport, neither among gluttonous eaters of flesh.

[21] For women who are drunkards and are always at the wine table and are gluttonous, many waste their life on frivolous activities. They

shall come to ruin, and if her eyelids remain drowsy, her body shall be clothed with rags.

✤ Be a Good Steward ✤

[22] Hearken unto your father who begat you, and despise not your mother because of her years, for she has traveled on before you and knows the dangers.

[23] Buy the truth, and sell it not, for it has with it wisdom and instruction and understanding. They will aid you by making you aware of the detestability of lies.

[24] The father of a righteous woman shall greatly rejoice, and she who begets wise children shall have joy because of them.

[25] Your father and your mother shall be glad, because you have made being successful your goal and achieved your goal of a good life, and for that, they shall rejoice as one soul.

[26] My daughter, give unto Adonai your attention and watch for His direction and take note of His attributes and do likewise.

[27] Know that a whorish man is like a deep ditch and a strange man is a narrow pit, a godly man is faithful, and a scoundrel can be a chameleon. Which would you like?

[28] A deceitful man lies in wait and seeks and asks for prey and will commit many transgressions against women; a good man is honorable. Which would you like?

✤ Things to lose ✤

[29] Who has woe? Who has sorrow? Who has contentions? Who has babblings? Who has wounds without cause? Who has redness of eyes?

[30] Who are they? They are those who stay long at the table drinking wine. Therefore, my daughter, drink not much wine, for there are many who drink just to keep from having inadequate

feelings. And for many, their gulps are deep, for they seek to escape trouble. And they who seek mixed wine desires to be a fatality.

[31] Wine is much desired because it is sweet, and while it is red, it is inviting and enticing as it gives off its color in the cup. All the while it is there lying still; it's waiting for you.

[32] At last, like a serpent, it bites and stings from within the blood.

[33] Then, my daughter, your eyes shall behold strange men and your heart shall share its secrets because you chose to utter perverse private things.

[34] Yea, you shall be like her who lies down in the midst of the sea of lusts and like a foolish woman who places herself in dangerous situations believing it to be a pleasure, inviting trouble.

[35] She says, "The wine has stricken me, because I was not sick in my body but was surely bruised by it. It has caused doubts about me and my name, and I knew it not. But when I awake, I will return to it again!"

[36] My daughter, know that that which ails you, your mother suffers the same ailment. Your mother, like God, only desires for you to be happy, so listen to her wisdom.

24

Have Good Intentions

[1] She who is righteous should not be envious of an ungodly and wicked woman and neither desire to be her companion but be ready to help.

[2] For a woman to cause harm, in her heart, she must first have thought about being destructive, and from her lips, she speaks of making mischief.

[3] A woman by wisdom can build and establish a house upon righteousness, and if she has understanding and attempts to avoid evil, it will remain sturdy.

[4] And only by the knowledge of wisdom shall a woman's chambers be filled with untainted, precious, and pleasant treasures for her to enjoy and to share with others.

[5] A wise woman is strong in character; therefore, a woman of knowledge will increase the strength of other women.

[6] She who has wise counsel is able to make war only a passing thought, and within a multitude of counselors, safety is assured.

[7] Wisdom is too heavy for a fool because it is cumbersome, and she who opens her mouth without control is likened to a tumbling rock. Therefore, she will not be given any responsibility.

Unwise

[8] She who is mischievous beyond normal shall be called devilish, and her soul shall be hanging in the balance.

[9] The thoughts of sin will lead to foolishness and more sin, and the wayward soul is an abomination to God and a shame to other women.

[10] She who has fear and faints in the face of adversity will do so because she thinks she is weak.

[11] Give heed and do not forbear to deliver them who are being executed unjustly, and for those who are ready to be slain, speak on their behalf.

[12] If you say, "Behold, I knew it not," Adonai who ponders the heart considers it. Yes, He who keeps your soul is wise. Yes, He knows and shall render to every woman according to her works.

[13] My daughter, honey is sweet and good. Together with the honeycomb, it is sweeter. It will help you to know the taste of bitterness.

[14] Great shall the knowledge of wisdom be to the soul of a woman. And when you find it, there shall be a reward of self-satisfaction that has no equal, and your expectation shall be ongoing and not shortened.

❧ God Sees All ❧

[15] A thief will plan and wait for an opportunity to move against the unsuspecting. Therefore, O wicked woman, seek not for an opportunity to go against her who is vulnerable, for God is her avenger.

[16] Look upon her who is a just woman and notice how she fell down seven times and yet she rises up again; also know that her strength lies in the Lord. But the wicked shall fall into mischief continuously and will not have strength enough to get out, for they trust not in Adonai.

¹⁷ Rejoice not when your enemy falls, and let not your heart be glad when she stumbles.

¹⁸ Lest the Lord see it and it displeases Him and He turns away His wrath from her.

¹⁹ My daughter, worry not yourself because of evil women; neither be you envious of their ways.

²⁰ For the wicked woman's reward shall be according to her works, and for her wickedness, she will be like a short-stemmed candle and shall go out presently.

²¹ My daughter, fear the Lord and His rulers and your mother and father and neither intermeddle nor intermingle with them who give in to the winds of change for self-satisfaction.

²² My daughter, whimsical fantasies cause calamities, for they are as unpredictable as the weather. Because attitudes can change suddenly, not many rulers can understand nor will they know how much life will suffer or change because of it.

❧ Being On Guard ❧

²³ The things that are defined as good belong unto the wise children of God; therefore, it is not good to have respect of persons in judgment.

²⁴ She who is in power and says unto the wicked, "Your ways are just," her own people shall curse her and other leaders shall isolate themselves from her.

²⁵ But to them who rebuke her, they shall receive the appreciation of her friends, because to them, a time of rejoicing is at hand.

²⁶ Every woman shall kiss her lips that gives a right answer, because it comes from the heart and it is sweet.

²⁷ Prepare yourself for life, for only by preparation and accommodation can you make yourself ready for it—first, by sowing your seeds in the field, and afterward, by building your house.

²⁸ My daughter, do not be a deceiver; neither lie nor cause harm to be done against your neighbor.

²⁹ Say not "I will do so to her as she has done to me." Remember, Adonai will render to a woman according to her works and to yours.

❧ Lost ❧

³⁰ My daughter, as I went by the marketplaces and found there them who refused to do any labor, I also saw the vineyard of the woman who was void of the necessary skills, and they all were deprived of labors wisdom in order to make a living.

³¹ I also saw how she was unlike other merchants with goods, and unlike them she had no goods to sell, yet she had carts. And I saw that her appearance seemed to be like an unkempt field that became overgrown with rubbish and like unpicked fruit that had begun to rot. Shame had covered her face, and her spirit appeared to have been broken.

³² As I continued to gaze and ponder upon these women, I saw and considered the cause, and it bothered me. Then my father's words were made evident that a person's life can be like a field if their life is not cared, for it will be had in shambles.

³³ Therefore, their life reflected back at them as if it were out of focus, because they preferred a little sleep and a little relaxing slumber and with lazy hands that can only hold each other as they were feeble and refused to pick up the tools to learn and labor. That is why their life echoed failure.

³⁴ Poverty shall appear to a woman and come upon her as an advancing army. And like an armed woman in need of prey to satisfy her hunger yet finding none, so, too, shall that woman be in need of peace but finding it not.

25

Advice for Queens

[1] The wisdom of Solomon, which, if he had a daughter, he would have shared with her.

[2] It is God's privilege and honor to conceal much regarding His great glory, but the honor of queens and kings is to search out a matter for their own honor and their own good.

[3] The heaven for height and the earth for depth and the heart of queens and kings regarding their decisions are unsearchable.

[4] Take away the dross from the silver, and there shall come forth a vessel fit for precious things. Therefore, my daughter, settle not for a little refining.

[5] Take away the advice of the wicked, and what is left is good counsel. And the queen's throne shall be established upon righteous judgments.

[6] A false image is not real beauty; neither is presenting this image before important women, for they are wise.

[7] When your own pride causes you to assume a place of honor in the presence of the queen because you thought it was a right, know that when you are asked to step down and leave from being in her presence, shame will follow. Therefore, desire the fellowship of equals first. For it is better that it be said unto you, "Come up hither."

[8] Go not forth hastily to a judge for a settlement to shame your neighbor, and if you are found to be a liar, shame shall be heaped upon you instead.

[9] She who shares her feelings with someone who is considered a confidant does so in trust, and she who betrays that trust is unjust, so chose your friends wisely.

[10] Therefore, if she hears your secret and then shares it with others, she does so knowing that she has betrayed your trust in her. Therefore, she will cause you embarrassment, and you shall be known as having an infamous character.

[11] My daughter, a word that is fitly spoken at the opportune moment is as sweet as golden nectar served in a silver picture. Therefore, are not just words more desirable?

[12] As an earring of gold will shimmer and glisten, and an ornament of fine gold is even shinier, so is a wise reproof upon an obedient ear.

[13] As the refreshing rain before the time of harvest is beneficial, so, too, is a faithful messenger to them who send her, for her actions are just and acceptable to those who send her.

[14] She who is boastful of her beauty and is deceitful can be compared to a grouping of threatening clouds and wind without rain and will leave no benefit behind.

[15] As a soft tongue breaks through the barrier of despair, so, too, can a princess be persuaded by continual attendance on just matters.

❧ Conscientious Actions ❧

[16] If you find some honey, eat so much as is sufficient for you, lest you be filled therewith and vomit it. Therefore, be moderate in all things!

[17] Withdraw your foot from your neighbor's house, lest she becomes weary of your long and frequent visits, and then she will hate you.

[18] A woman who bears false witness against her neighbor is appalling.

¹⁹ Confidence in an unfaithful woman in time of trouble is like a ruined garment and a foot out of joint.

²⁰ She who has a heavy heart, no amount of rejoicing can lift the sorrow off it.

²¹ If your enemy is hungry, give her bread to eat, and if she is thirsty, give her water to drink.

²² For you shall awaken her conscience from its sleep, and the Lord shall reward you.

²³ The north wind will surely drive away rain, and an angry countenance drives away a backbiting tongue.

²⁴ It is better to dwell in the corner of the house behind a door in silence than openly around a brawling man within a wide house.

²⁵ As a cold drink of water is refreshing to a thirsty body, so is good news from a far country to your spirit.

²⁶ If a woman who is perceived to be righteous and she is then shown to be corrupt by kneeling down before the wicked, it can surely be troubling to just women. And because she lacked integrity and good judgment, like a corrupt spring that just bubbles, she will be unable to uplift your spirit, for her shame is of her own doing.

²⁷ It is not good to eat too much honey, and for a woman to search her own glory is not glory, for she will excuse her own actions as being right.

²⁸ She who has no self-control or is unable to rule over her own spirit is like a city that is bound to be conquered because it lacks the protections of a wall.

²⁹ My daughter, as a candle in a darkened room is comforting, so shall the love of God be to you if He dwells in your heart.

26

All about Fools

[1] As snow in summer and rain with no clouds causes confusion; therefore, to honor a fool is not wise.

[2] As the bird by wandering and the swallow by flying will bring no harm to the air, and for a woman to just wish it cannot cause another's life to face decay.

[3] A whip for the horse, a bridle for the ass, and strong actions against a fool will surely cause no harm.

[4] Answer not a fool according to her folly, for she may feign ignorance, lest you also be like her, a conceited fool.

[5] Be ready to answer a fool according to her folly, for perspicuous ignorance is unjust. Share with her the instruction of wisdom, lest she be wise in her own conceits.

[6] For a woman to send a message of great importance by a fool is similar to poisoning a good well, causing much damage.

[7] She who puts words of wisdom in a fool's mouth is similar to placing two equal columns on unequal ground.

[8] For a woman to join herself to a fool is not wise, for they both shall achieve a dishonored reputation.

[9] It is not wise to place a weapon in the hand of someone who drinks too much wine; it can also be said that parables in the mouth of fools are of no consequence.

[10] The great God who formed all things will surely reward the fool with folly, and He will also reward transgressors with adversity.

[11] As a dog returns to its vomit, so does a fool returns to his or her folly, ignoring the voice of reason.

[12] If you meet a woman who is conceited, there is more hope of a fool than of her.

[13] The slothful woman will always excuse her behavior by saying "There is a lion in the way" as a reason not to venture forth to erase her hunger.

[14] As the door turns upon it's hinges, so will the slothful upon her bed, because there is a lion in the street.

[15] The slothful hides her hands in her bosom; it grieves her to bring them to her mouth. Therefore, her soul shall die from lack of food.

❧ Avoiding Wisdom ❧

[16] The sluggard is vain and conceited and believes her actions are just; therefore, she will reject the wisdom of seven women who can render a reason for her to be successful.

[17] My daughter, she who takes a wolf by the ears seeks misgivings, for it will turn on her. Therefore, do not go meddling in another's marriage, bringing harm to yourself.

[18] A madwoman can be like a fiery arrow causing more than death, and she who acts like a lumbering elephant will cause much harm.

[19] Her actions can be as destructive as locusts, which only seek to feed themselves, so for a woman who goes about to deceive her neighbor and then says "I meant no harm, for it was only in jest" is not good.

[20] Where no wood is, surely the fire goes out. So where there is no instigator, strife ceases.

[21] As fresh coals are added to burning coals to keep a fire burning, so, too, is wood added to fire for warmth. therefore a contentious and abusive woman be able to kindle strife.

[22] She who is a teller of lies is like a wound that will not heal; thereby lies can also affect the belly.

[23] Burning lips that speaks lies and a heart that is known to be wicked are as valuable as a broken pot that is covered with gold but holds no water.

[24] She who hates others will hide it with fair speech. Within her words, there lies deceit, and by her actions, she will bring hurt.

[25] My daughter, be aware of her whose words are always fair; believe her not. For within her heart there lies some of these traits—a spirit of fornication, lasciviousness, idolatry, wantonness, witchcraft, wrath, strife, and drunkenness.

[26] Her hatred is covered by deceit. Eventually, all her lies shall become exposed, and her true nature is revealed for all to see.

[27] Be careful as to the type of storm you brew; it may cause you to fall into the hole you dug.

[28] A lying tongue will ruin those who are afflicted by it, and a flattering mouth works ruin, so choose not to be boisterous.

[29] My daughter, having joy in life invites more of the same, so does sorrow, and a fool is sure to be alone.

27

Cause and Effect

¹ She who says she knows what will happen tomorrow is wicked, because only Adonai knows what is truly going to happen, and He alone has the power to change things.

² Let another woman praise you and not your own voice; it is better for a stranger to speak well of you and not your own lips.

³ A boulder and water together has great weight, but she who is wronged, her wrath is heavier than them both.

⁴ Wrath is cruel, and anger is outrageous, but who is able to stand before the ways of an envious person?

⁵ She who is unjust, rebuke and fear not that you may lose her love.

⁶ Faithful words from a friend sometimes causes wounds. Although she attempts to understand your pain and tries to help by providing guidance, it seems to cause hurt, but beware of the kisses of someone who is neither a friend nor an enemy.

⁷ She who is full will leave the honeycomb on the table. As a woman of understanding, she will know when to say enough, but to the hungry soul that yearns for pleasures, even a rotten apple is sweet.

⁸ A daughter who leaves her home before her time is similar to a yearling that goes astray, not knowing the dangers.

⁹ Ointment and perfume rejoice the heart, so does the sweetness of a woman's friend by her hearty counsel.

[10] It is better for a woman to have a good friend who is near than a relative who is far away when trouble comes; also keep close friends that are your own and those of your mother's.

[11] My daughter, be wise so that I may have joy regarding you, so that when my neighbor comes to give reproach, I will have a reason to have a glad heart by which I may answer her.

[12] A prudent woman foresees the evil and will keep herself from it, but the simple pass on and are punished forthwith.

[13] She who puts up her possessions as a security for payment for her who is a friend does so for the sake of friendship. Therefore, if her friend refuses to restore the pledge given to her, then her possessions will be forfeited.

[14] She who rises early and goes about in the community and speaks good of her neighbor with a loud voice shall not make many friends, for they shall curse her for it, so be careful of much praise giving.

[15] Is it good for a woman to know that her spirit can be compared to a thunderous and stormy rain that seems to have no end and it is her husband that thinks so?

[16] He may seek to silence her but thinks, *Can I silence the noise of the wind?* Like oil in the hand, she will not be corralled, not even by her husband.

[17] The reward for grace given is grace bestowed, and it is by grace that she is made able to understand that true love is given from a loving heart.

[18] Whosoever is the keeper of the fig tree shall eat the fruit as a reward, and she who is a good companion to her mistress and waits on her instructions shall be honored in due time.

[19] As a woman looks upon and sees her reflection in a mirror, that woman's heart can also be reflected back, for it will reveal her true intentions to her.

[20] Hell is never full, and a fire, if given fuel, will not cease. So, too, are the eyes of a woman, for they are never satisfied.

[21] As the fining pot is for silver and the furnace for gold, so, too, can a woman's character be defined by what is said of her.

²² She who is wise will be so because the rubbish that comes from wicked thoughts was removed by a little sifting of foreign ideas, but the foolish will not let go of folly and neither be removed from foolishness no matter how often they are reproved.

²³ Be diligent to know the state of your property, and look well to sustain your business with more opportunities, or come to know failure and poverty instead.

²⁴ Riches are not meant to last forever; therefore, a gold crown that is passed on will not endure without much care.

❧ God and You ❧

²⁵ God's goodwill is that the hay in the field and the tender grass appear for both beauty and food; therefore, women are meant to be beautiful and to labor as much as men, for they are also to gather much of their fruits from off the mountains and in the valleys.

²⁶ God does surely look toward the needs of all people by providing the earth seed, water, and sun. He gives strength to the workers and provides animals for labor, along with food and clothing, so that they can want for nothing. Selah.

²⁷ And by your work, you shall have cheeses and breads and fruits and dwellings enough for yourself and your own workers besides. This is a soul's portion as directed by God.

²⁸ My daughter, as your child grows, so shall her love for you, but one misspoken word and she will be angry at you. But in time she shall learn that love is fair and love you again.

²⁹ It is always a wise thing to give and show understanding no matter the cause for the anger.

28

Conscientious Rules

¹ The wicked will flee and run and hide, imagining that they are being chased, although no one is pursuing after them. But the righteous are as bold as a lion, for their actions are of merit.

² A woman of state who acts foolishly, causing much confusion in the presence of others, shall have many adversaries. However, a woman of understanding and knowledge ensures the stability of the state, and it will be prolonged.

³ A poor woman who oppresses the poor is surely unjust in her ways; she can be like a sweeping rain that destroys a crop.

⁴ They who forsake the law are on the side of the wicked that go about mischievously in a community, but whosoever keeps the law fights against them in proper fashion.

⁵ Evil women understand not righteous judgments that are given against them, but they who seek the Lord understand righteousness and more.

⁶ She who is perverse in her ways, whether she be rich or poor, dishonors her God. But she who keeps His commandments walks with dignity and, by having a fair spirit, does gracefully honor her God.

⁷ She who keeps the law of her father is a wise dignified daughter, but she who is a companion of riotous women shames her father and mother.

⁸ She who lends a little to the poor and exacts much in return to increase her substance is unjust; she will soon realize that all her efforts shall become as meaningless as a gnat. Therefore, shall she see the poor honoring another who has taken that which she has and shared it with others.

⊰❧ A Good Path ❧⊱

⁹ She who turns away her ear from hearing the law of goodwill, even her prayers, shall be an abomination unto Adonai.

¹⁰ She who is misleading to the righteous and causes them to go astray unto an evil path shall herself fall into her own pit, but the uprightness of the upright shall preserve them, and they shall retain blessings.

¹¹ The rich woman believes that her riches will make her wise. Therefore, she is conceited, but she who is spiritually rich knows that the heart is deceitful, for she has searched it out.

¹² When righteous women do rejoice, there is great glory for all to share, but when the wicked rise, wise women are told to hide, for the wicked seeks to mock them.

¹³ She who covers her sins shall not prosper, but whoso confesses and forsakes them shall obtain mercy through grace.

¹⁴ Happy is the woman who always fears to venture onto dark paths, but she who hardens her heart charges onward, seeing mischief as a way of life, and shall fall into a darkened pit.

¹⁵ As a roaring lioness seeking its prey and a ranging bear seeking her cubs, and she who is a wicked ruler and has authority over poor people, she too can be implacable.

¹⁶ She who is a ruler and taxes her people to fill her coffers is unjust, lacks wisdom, and brings ruin to all, and because of vanity and covetousness, her days as a ruler will not be prolonged.

❧ Self-Destruction ❦

¹⁷ A woman who commits violence upon the being of any person shall attempt to flee the judgment of her own conscience but cannot find anyone who can help her.

¹⁸ Whoso walks upright shall deliver their soul from destruction, but she who is perverse in her ways shall fall down hard without any help.

❧ Good Intensions ❦

¹⁹ She who has an industrious spirit shall have her future secured, but she who follows after unruly people and is slothful shall have poverty as a companion.

²⁰ A faithful woman shall abound with blessings, but she who makes haste to be rich shall not be innocent of lusting.

²¹ For a woman to have respect of a person for the purpose of business is not good, because she desires a bribe; thereby that woman shall commit a transgression.

²² She who is in want of much more than she has will chase after more, not being satisfied; neither does she consider that poverty is also chasing her. So be content.

²³ She who rebukes a wise woman shall afterward receive favor for herself, but she who considers a flattering tongue as a form of wisdom is foolish.

²⁴ Whoso robs her father or her mother and says it is no transgression, the same is the companion of a destroyer.

²⁵ She who has a vain spirit does not mind causing trouble, but she who puts her trust in the Lord shall have a great soul adjourned with a good life.

²⁶ She who trusts in her own heart without Adonai's guidance is a fool, but she who walks wisely knowing her heart is deceitful shall be delivered from many misgivings.

[27] She who gives unto the poor shall not be lacking or wanting for any good thing, because she has many blessings, but she who hides her eyes and withholds her hand from the needy invites poverty.

[28] When a wicked man comes, good women should hide, for he seeks their riches. But when the wicked perish, then their riches shall increase and their virtue shall be seen in the youth who are educated.

[29] My daughter, good judgment and righteousness are sure to guide you into everlasting success, but an unruly spirit is folly, for it is without discretion and it is doomed.

29

Consequences

¹ She who is often reproved shall stiffen her resolve against those who seek her good, but for a lack of knowledge, she shall suddenly be disillusioned, and there shall be no one to help.

² When a righteous woman is in authority, she is fair, and the people will rejoice. But when she is wicked, her own interests are paramount, and the people mourn.

³ She who loves wisdom rejoices with her father, but she who keeps company with harlots and whorish men and women wastes her substance.

⁴ The queen, by good judgment, established the land, but she who receives bribes is sure to bring many burdens upon the land and people.

⁵ A woman who knowingly flatters her neighbor to gain an advantage will set a trap for herself.

⁶ An evil woman will deceive you in order to catch you in a trap, but she who is righteous will sing and rejoice because she evaded the snare that was set to destroy her spiritual character.

⁷ Righteous women will consider the causes of the poor, but the wicked will look upon the poor and have no regard.

⁸ A woman who's in a position of authority and is scornful will bring corruption to a fine city, but wise women will instead watch

for deceptive practices of certain people and will turn those people away.

⁹ If a wise woman contends with a foolish woman and then settles the matter between them, then the foolish woman may laugh out of frustration.

¹⁰ The righteous woman will forgive them who sought to cause her harm for the sake of her own soul.

¹¹ A fool utters all her mind prior to knowing the cause, but a wise woman will keep her words till she hears the whole matter.

¹² When a wicked ruler has advisers who are wicked, then her judgments are a result of their advice.

¹³ When the selfish and the unselfish woman meet together, the Lord shall provide enlightenment to both their eyes.

¹⁴ The queen who faithfully judges all her people equally, her kingdom shall prosper in her lifetime and beyond because she has established a good foundation.

¹⁵ Addressing a child in an appropriate manner will produce goodwill, but a child left to him or herself brings the mother to shame and a father to despair.

¹⁶ When the wicked are multiplied, there will be many transgressions; therefore, the righteous shall view the fall of the wicked.

¹⁷ Correct your daughter, and she shall give your conscience rest. Yea, surely your soul shall be delighted by her.

¹⁸ My daughter, if you have no vision of your future, your future is bleak and your children will suffer also. In order to be happy, go and seek Adonai's guidance.

¹⁹ She who is stubborn will not be corrected because you speak affectionately; even though she understands that you care, she will not change.

²⁰ If you look upon a woman who is anxious, she will be hasty in uttering words for no reason and will give up her virtue. Some may say, "There is more hope of a fool than of her."

²¹ She who raises a child with a stern heart and with love, wisdom, and encouragement, she shall gain a true daughter and an heir.

²² An angry woman who will stir up strife causes hatred, and a furious woman's transgressions will grow to become outrageous.

²³ A woman's pride shall bring about her downfall, but through honor and grace and a humble spirit, her support shall come from just women.

²⁴ She who is a partner with a thief is not being fair to her own soul, and she, unknowingly, seeks a loss of liberty, thereby having heard the plans of the wicked and refusing to let them be known she is to be judged equally guilty.

²⁵ Fear not a wicked woman because she states she can bring you harm, but instead believe that Adonai can ensure your safety, because her words have no power over you.

²⁶ For the queen's favor, many will give gifts. It is wise to know that Adonai's favor is not brought but sought, and He will reward you for it.

²⁷ An unjust woman is disgusting and hated and is an abomination to the just; even her acquaintances find fault in her. But she who is justified by Adonai will be appreciated for her spirit. The exception is that the wicked shall find her to be an abomination.

²⁸ A mule that is joined to an ox has no choice but turn when it turns; it is also true of a woman who has for a friend someone who has influence over her.

30

The Daughter of a Wise Man

¹ The words of Ches'mine, the daughter of a wise man, shares her writings with others.

² Surely I am somewhat of a foolish woman, yet I stand as an equal to all. Yea, I also may not be as like-minded or have all the understanding of a man or woman.

³ I neither learned nor obtained wisdom from fools, nor do I have all the knowledge of the Holy One.

⁴ For I know of no one who has ascended up into heaven or descended into Sheol nor anyone who has gathered the wind in their fists or who can put water in a rock or who could have established all the ends of the earth. Do you know someone who claims this right? And if you know, then tell me the name of that person so I also may know.

⁵ Every word of God is pure, just, and holy, and He stands as a shield for everyone who puts their trust in Him.

⁶ Add not unto His words in order to increase its value and your own, lest you have to prove what you say to be true about Him and you be found a liar.

⁷ My Father, two things I have required of you: deny me them not before I die.

[8] Let not a truly vain attitude overcome me so that lies will become my reality. Give me neither total poverty nor total riches. Feed me with substance that is convenient for my well-being.

[9] Lest my soul be unequal and I deny you by saying, "Who is this Adonai?" Or lest I be poor and steal or be rich and want more and then take the name of my God in vain.

[10] Accuse not a servant unto her mistress, lest she bring an accusation against you and you be found guilty.

✥ Just Actions ✥

[11] There is a generation that curses their father and will not honor their mother for selfish reasons.

[12] There is another generation that considers themselves to be just and pure in their own eyes, deceiving and being deceived, yet they have not been washed from their filthiness, for they remain vain and are lacking a reason to have a clean heart.

[13] I know of another generation of people who believe that they are above all others and will treat you with contempt; they will look upon you as if you were dung, for they have no respect for others. Yet, they, like you, were created by God.

[14] There is another generation whose words are like swords and their jaw teeth like knives to set upon the poor of the earth to slash them, and their language, like a snake's tongue, will seek you out. I know that they do dwell among women just to oppress others; therefore, I choose not to be like them.

✥ Know When to Say Enough ✥

[15] I know and saw that the undisciplined have many a daughter crying "Give, give" and many a son crying "Needy, needy." Also know that there are three things that are never satisfied. Yea, four things say not it is enough:

¹⁶ The grave waiting to be filled, a womb awaiting to be filled, the earth that soaks in water, and the fire that continues to search for something to burn, for they all will not say enough.

¹⁷ She who has a wicked eye is despicable. Therefore, the ravens of the valley shall pick it out and the young eaglets shall eat it, for she has made a mockery of her father's words and failed to obey her mother, being undisciplined. She does not understand that her life is destined to decay.

⊶❧ Show Interest ❧⊷

¹⁸ My father tells me that there are three things that are even too wonderful for him to understand and a fourth that he knows can only exist in love:

¹⁹ The way of an eagle in the air and how it holds the wind, the way of a serpent upon a rock and why it does not slip, the way of a heavy ship in the midst of the sea, and the ways of a married couple.

²⁰ Many people spoke to me, and I became aware of the ways of an adulterous soul that will allow itself to indulge its animal nature, and because it is not satisfied, it will go looking for more conquests. Then afterward, it will go home and say, "I have done no wickedness."

²¹ For three things the earth is disquieted, and the fourth will cause it to quake.

²² When a servant is put in place with charges and not having guidance, her actions then become inexcusable, and she who eats and drinks, once full, will then act foolishly and spout curses.

²³ When a spiteful and hateful woman who feels she is unworthy is married, she will frustrate her husband, because she loves not her soul. And a maid who is heir to her mistress, she will cause much to be undone.

²⁴ I know there are four things that are little upon the earth, which we give little attention to or ponder, but they are exceedingly wiser than some people, and that is how I learned to be an achiever.

[25] The ants are a people not strong but are many, working to gather food to enable their survival in the winter.

[26] And rabbits know that they are weak and feeble creatures, and because they are aware of diverse dangers, they will make their dens among the rocks.

[27] The locusts have no king or true leader, yet they go forth, all of them, as one band with a purpose.

[28] The spider takes hold with its hands and is found in palaces, yet others fail to enter because they will give up.

[29] I can think of four things that when they are considered, they can be appreciated for their majesty, thereby, learned I lessons in humility.

[30] "A lioness," which is the matriarch among beasts and turns not away for any.

[31] "A whale" in the ocean, will swim free and "a horse," which is a stout creature will run without a care, and "a good queen" who knows her worth and that of her army. She will stand tall like the horns on a bull, and so, too, will you if you know your own spiritual worth.

[32] If you have done foolishly in lifting up yourself or if you have thought evil, place your hand upon your mouth and go and seek to humble yourself before your God, for humility is a majestic trait, and if it is fit for queens, then it is fit for all women.

[33] Surely the churning of milk brings forth butter and the wringing of the nose brings forth blood, and to bring forth strife upon your own head, use strife.

[34] Love understands and will forgive, but hate has its own reward.

31

Good Advice

¹ The words of a good father can also be heard by and addressed to a queen.

² O daughter of my loins and the daughter of my vows!

³ Give not your strength unto wicked men or your prudent ways to anything that will alter your queenly behavior and ruin your life.

⁴ It is not fit for queens, O my daughter; it is not fit for queens to drink wine or for princesses to partake of a strong drink.

⁵ Lest she drink and forget the law of her conscience and pervert the judgment of any of the afflicted.

⁶ A woman may give a strong drink unto her who is confused and ready to perish, and wine may be given unto those who are of heavy hearts, but beware because they may act foolishly.

⁷ In order for her to forget her sadness, let her drink a little wine and then console her, whereby she may remember her misery no more.

⁸ For a just and righteous cause, let your voice be heard for all those who may be treated in an unjust manner and are thereby appointed for ruin.

⁹ She who has to pass judgment should refrain herself from too much talk. To be sure, she must weigh the words of others righteously, then she shall plead the cause of the just and needy.

❧ Carefulness, Not Carelessness ❧

[10] My daughter, all men will seek to find a virtuous woman and will justifiably pay the price for her, because he knows the value of a good woman, and any woman will not due.

[11] My daughter, a husband's heart is confident and will safely trust in his wife, for her love is reserved for him so that he shall have no need of spoil.

[12] She will do him good and not evil all the days of her life, and he will do her justice all the days of his life.

[13] A good man seeks work and will work willingly and diligently with his hands to provide for and make her life and that of his children secure.

[14] He reminds her of a merchant ship that is homeward bound and brings many good things to enjoy, along with the necessities of life.

[15] She also rises while it is yet night and seeks and prepares sustenance for her household from that which he brought home to his loved ones.

[16] She considers an opportunity of value and shares it with him, and they shall work together to achieve their goals. Through the labor of her hands, she makes it prosperous like a vineyard, and they will enjoy the fruit thereof.

[17] She tightens a belt around her loins and dresses her hair, then she strengthens her arms and prepares for the work ahead. Nearby, her husband shall be laboring in the fields.

[18] She perceives that her ideas and merchandise is good and will work for a time to ensure its success, all the while not neglecting her husband's needs, and neither shall he neglect hers.

[19] She places her hands to the plow in order to obtain some value, and he will help to hold the distaff beside her, for they know that together they are strong.

[20] She will stretch out her hands to those in need. Yea, she reaches forth with her hands to join in the work with others, and her husband is proud.

²¹ He is not afraid of the changing seasons, for his wife will ensure that his household is clothed by working wisely. Therefore, the needs of their children are ensured because of their diligence.

²² Because he makes God his source for his needs, she also knows that her family is covered by grace; therefore, her family's garments were obtained through her labors and her raiment is fit for a queen.

²³ His wife is known in the gates as a graceful woman, and when she sits among the patriarchs and matriarchs of the land, they respectfully honor her.

²⁴ She is skillful and wise and has gained the knowledge of wise women and is able to provide to merchants her fashioned goods. Others seek her guidance for their endeavors so that they also may prosper.

²⁵ She, by youthful vigor and honor, which she wears as a dressing, and by being diligent now, shall rejoice in time to come.

²⁶ When she opens her mouth, her words are nourishing and full of wisdom, and the words across her tongue are kind.

²⁷ Her husband lives to ensure his family is taught the ways of God by being watchful and sober. Therefore, he works with the spirit and is not idle.

²⁸ Her children will get up early and are happy. Along with her husband, they will consider themselves blessed, for they have placed their trust in Adonai's teachings.

²⁹ My daughter, have a virtuous spirit along with strength of character, and you will be included with them nice women because you married a man who feared the Lord.

³⁰ Daughter, having a visage of beauty that is pleasing to the eye is good, but it will not last. But if a woman has a truthful spirit and in her heart she fears the Lord, she shall be praised for her beauty and that by her husband whose strength is also decreasing, and her desire for her children is from that same spirit.

³¹ Daughter, pray to God for your own soul with fear, lest you take the name of your God in vain, so that the fruit of your labor is

glorious. Therefore, your own works shall glorify you, and they will bring you into the company of wonderful women.

[32] My daughter, as your husband reaches to embrace you, reach for his hand and wrap it around you because he seeks your tenderness and because your beauty is always foremost in his heart.

FINISHED

Bibliography

The many different versions of the Bible were used to complete a main idea, and the references were derived from the following materials: NIV, ESV, God's Word Translation, Easy-to-Read Version, Complete Jewish Bible, the Darby Bible, and other works that are currently written in and produced commercially and digitized by Biblesoft Inc. (Copyright © 1988–2011, Biblesoft, all rights reserved). Reference materials were also contained within the Biblesoft material, Barnes's *Notes*, Electronic Database (Copyright © 1997, 2003, 2005, 2006 by Biblesoft Inc., all rights reserved). Resources for commentaries were taken from Adam Clark, Matthew Henry, Jamieson-Fausset-Brown, Barnes' *Notes*, and *The Teachers Commentary*, along with others commentaries that were derived from PC Study Bible and Biblesoft Inc. (Copyright © 1988–2011, Biblesoft, all rights reserved).

Other works and studies were also used as references and were not infringed upon or copied out, and any copyrighted text not listed here are not used. The commentaries referenced were used as they were intended for study; therefore, I used them to write a more clear thought on the verses that were written and referenced by Solomon and reprinted in the King James Version to provide an instructional form of writing of the different subjects and observations and other materials, which allowed me to have an original thought and provide my own insights and opinions to write this book without using any copyrighted/dated material.

Revised on February 24, 2021

Index

Lightning Source UK Ltd.
Milton Keynes UK
UKHW041937150321
380411UK00009B/1141/J